IN SEARCH OF AFRICA

PEOPLE AND PLACES OF THE WORLD

IN SEARCH

OF

AFRICA

Reader's
Digest

PUBLISHED BY THE READER'S DIGEST ASSOCIATION LIMITED

LONDON   NEW YORK   MONTREAL   SYDNEY   CAPE TOWN

Originally published in partwork form,
Des Pays et des Hommes,
by Librairie Larousse, Paris

Contents

COVER PICTURES

Top: *The volcanic cone of Mount Kilimanjaro in Tanzania
is Africa's highest mountain. It rises to a height of 19,340 feet.*
Bottom: *These Samburu girls from Kenya wear traditional brightly coloured beads.*

Africa: Continent of a Thousand Tongues

According to the traditions of the Fulani herdsmen of Mali in West Africa, the world began as a huge drop of milk. Then came the god Doondari and he created stone. Stone created iron, which created fire, which created water, which created air. Doondari then appeared a second time and used the five elements to fashion man. Unfortunately, man became proud, so Doondari was obliged to create blindness, 'and blindness defeated man'. But then blindness also became proud, and so Doondari had to create sleep in order to defeat blindness. Sleep became too proud and Doondari created worry. Worry went the same way and was dealt with by death. When, finally, death became too proud, Doondari descended for the third time. This time he came as Gueno, the eternal one, and defeated death.

Africa's stories of gods and men and of how the world was formed are as varied as its tribes and peoples. Indeed, a continent where anything between 800 and over 1000 different languages are spoken reveals a similar variety in just about every area of life. Its peoples range from the stately Masai warriors of the West African savanna to the tiny Pygmies of the Congo jungle; from the ancient tribes of Bushmen surviving in the Kalahari Desert to the mixed-race 'Bastars' of Namibia; from the oil-rich capitalists of Nigeria to the die-hard members of the the so-called 'white tribe' of the Afrikaners. In landscapes too, it encompasses astonishing contrasts such as those between the volcanic cone of Mount Kilimanjaro rising to permanently snow-capped heights only three degrees south of the Equator and the sun-baked, scrubby plains spreading around its feet; or between the Mediterranean-style luxuriance of the fruit and vine-clad valleys of the Cape in the south and the arid wildernesses of the Karoo just a few hundred miles inland.

The variety of its wildlife – the lions, elephants, giraffes, zebras, antelopes, hippopotamuses and rhinoceroses guarded against poachers and over-enthusiastic game hunters in a series of national parks and reserves – is, of course, famous. But equally there is the variety of human lifestyles, old and new, traditional and modern, mingling in a sometimes happy – though often less fortunate – confusion. An idea of its extent, and of the sufferings as well as the glories it has always involved, can be gained simply enough with a glance at a few of the continent's cities: Nairobi and Johannesburg, late 19th-century boom towns built on the profits of European colonial trade; Zanzibar, constructed on the exotic 'island of cloves' but once capital of an Arab slave-trading empire. In Zimbabwe stand the ruins that until the 19th century were the capital of the once-mighty, Bantu-speaking empire of Monomatapa.

The continent itself is constructed something like a vast craggy fortress. It consists for the most part of an enormous plateau of ancient hard rock raised on high escarpments that climb sharply from narrow coastal strips. These escarpments, preventing ready access to the interior, have for centuries formed one of Africa's best natural defences – not even the four great rivers, the Niger,

Congo, Zambezi and Nile, are easily navigable for much of their lengths, thanks to the series of waterfalls or cataracts where they tumble over the edges of the escarpments. In addition, the coast of Africa is also remarkably smooth, providing another line of defence, since it offers comparatively few bays or inlets to shelter the vessels of outsiders.

Once through to the interior, on the other hand, Africa presents few natural barriers to impede the coming and going of men or animals. The continent has experienced relatively little of the 'folding' effects of the movements of the Earth's surface that elsewhere in the world have thrown up great mountain ranges. It does, however, have one equally spectacular feature: the southern portions of the Great Rift Valley which stretches from eastern Turkey in the north, down the Red Sea, into Ethiopia and down through East Africa until it reaches the sea at the mouth of the Zambezi. Along its length are Africa's Great Lakes, such as Lake Victoria (covering a little under 27,000 square miles and the world's third largest lake) and Lake Nyasa; many of Africa's earliest fixed communities grew up around these lakes.

Men and men-like creatures (the ancestors of modern *Homo sapiens*) have dwelt on the African continent for millennia. According to scholars, the first of these (known as *Ramapithecus*) roamed East Africa some 14 million years ago. Then, a comparatively recent 5 million years ago, came the tool-making *Australopithecus*, traces of whom have been found in Tanzania and the Transvaal of South Africa. Neanderthal man, a hunter who used stone tools, emerged some 60,000 years ago and then, around 35,000 years ago, came the first settlements scattered through most of Africa of *Homo sapiens*, with the first farmers appearing around 5500 BC. During these early centuries the continent seems to have been populated fairly evenly by both yellow-skinned men and women (the ancestors of today's Bushmen and Khoikhoi) and the Negroid ancestors of today's black Africans. In the centuries leading up to around AD 1000, however, there appears to have been a shift in favour of the black Africans. Starting from the north-east of modern Nigeria, Bantu-speaking peoples, in particular, spread out over central, eastern and southern Africa until they dominated most of the southern third of the continent, with the Bushmen and their kin confined to the remoter corners of regions such as the Kalahari Desert and the Cape. At the same time, the knowledge and use of iron spread through most of Africa.

The Middle Ages saw the successive rise and fall of a number of African empires, the best known of which straddled the trade routes into and out of the southern Sahara. Ghana emerged as a great power in the 6th century AD, reaching its peak around 1000. Then came the Muslim realm of Mali whose greatest ruler was the Emperor Mansa Musa (1307-1332) – his capital was Niani but his most splendid city was Timbuctu, famed for its wealth, its unversities, libraries and traditions of scholarship. Mali was in turn succeeded by Songhai, another Muslim realm, on the banks of the Niger, which was at the height of its power and wealth at the end of the 15th century. In East Africa, meanwhile, Arab traders dealing in gold and slaves had established themselves in a chain of coastal settlements such as Mogadishu and Mombasa and laid the foundations of a distinctive Swahili (Arab-African) culture.

Then came the first incursions of the European powers. From the late 15th century onwards the Portuguese, Dutch and British started exploring the West African coast in particular, initially in search of the sea route to India, but then in pursuit of the 'black ivory' of slaves to work the plantations of the New World. This grim but profitable trade was responsible over the centuries for removing a possible 30-100 million Africans from their native continent – not including the millions exported by Arab slave-traders from East Africa. It also shifted the balance of power towards the forest kingdoms of Central Africa, such as Kongo, Ashanti and Dahomey, whose rulers were all too often happy to exchange slaves for European guns and other products. Comparatively safe in the high interior, realms such as Zimbabwe's Monomatapa and later in the 19th century the Zulu kingdom rose and fell, but the seclusion of inner Africa could not last for ever. In the mid-19th century the British missionary and impassioned anti-slaver David Livingstone was determined to open the interior to normal trade as a means of undercutting the profits of slaving. He and his fellows were extremely successful. The last decades of the 19th century saw the great 'Scramble for Africa' in which the European powers partitioned between them almost the entire continent. The European powers often settled their rival claims to territory by agreeing on rivers as boundaries or by drawing straight lines on the map – lines that took no account of the history and social traditions of the Africans. Nomads could be confined within frontiers, ethnic groups divided, others made uneasy bedfellows to suit the convenience of the chancelleries of Europe.

Africa today has to live with this heritage. Endowed on the one hand with a number of sources of wealth – not least huge mineral resources such as oil in Nigeria, copper in Zambia, diamonds, gold and plutonium in South Africa – it is yet bedevilled in many places with chronic political instability and economic mismanagement, not to mention the appalling scourges of disease and famine. The withdrawing European powers in the 1960s and 70s left societies whose traditional patterns and lines of authority had been hopelessly disrupted during colonial rule, but who encountered formidable problems in adapting to alternative forms of organisation, such as Western-style democracy. Their economies, meanwhile, were frequently dependent on the export of a handful of agricultural or mineral products (copper, coffee, groundnuts and so on), and thus extremely vulnerable to shifts in world markets. In South Africa, during the same period, the worst features of apartheid have been dismantled but the road to political and economic stability still looks difficult.

But then, of course, the Africans do have a remarkable gift of survival. Among their folktales, none remain more popular than those that recount the exploits of creatures such as Anansi – the spider hero of many West African tales, who has his counterparts in the tortoise and hare of tales in other parts of Africa. Anansi and his fellows are rarely paragons of virtue; indeed, they are usually downright tricksters. But they do have an exuberant shrewdness and earthy cunning that helps them to win against bigger and more powerful animals, and unfailingly captures the sympathies of the audience. Looking around the villages, markets, overloaded buses and noise-filled, colourful streets of modern Africa it is not hard to find similar examples of tenacity, shrewdness and the simple joy of living. For all its blights of disease, poverty and famine, Africa remains true to much of its traditional spirit and in this lies one of its chief hopes for the future.

South Africa

Situated at the tip of a vast continent, South Africa is a land of incredible
variety and major contrasts. More than a dozen different languages are spoken
within its borders, great wealth is juxtaposed with extreme poverty, and the landscape
itself ranges from parched desert in the west to lush, sub-tropical forest in the east.
With the sorry chapter of apartheid finally and mercifully closed,
South Africans are striving to build a future in which all can equally share
in the riches of this beautiful country.

Where buck may safely graze. The Kalahari Gemsbok National Park is an almost 4000-square-mile expanse of sandy terrain wedged between the borders of Namibia and Botswana in the far northern Cape interior. The great plains are sparsely but sweetly grassed, sustaining huge numbers of springbok and other animals.

The enchanting Montrose Falls tumble through the eastern Transvaal's Crocodile River valley near Schoemanskloof, the gateway from Highveld to Lowveld.

Preceding page: the Mother City. Visitors ascending Table Mountain enjoy breathtaking views of Cape Town and, beyond, of the harbour and bay.

Nature's Troubled Masterpiece

South Africa has an impressive abundance of natural gifts: formidable mineral riches, a kaleidoscopic array of scenic splendours, a benign climate and a wealth of wildlife that attracts hundreds of thousands of tourists annually from all over the world.

Yet there is an obverse side to this attractive picture, for the country has also been saddled with an unenviable burden of problems. Although the curtain has finally been rung down on the doomed policy of apartheid, the decision-makers of today are still tackling its legacy: the desperate need for more schools, more jobs, more houses, more hospitals – and how to narrow the cavernous income gap that exists between rich and poor.

South Africa's coat of arms, created at the nation's birth in 1910, carries the Latin legend *Ex Unitate Vires* – 'Strength from Unity'. It was an unlucky choice for a country where unity has, until very recently, been conspicuous by its absence. For if ever there has been a society divided against itself, it has been South Africa.

The coat of arms was created from the 'union' achieved in 1910 between the two former Boer republics of the Transvaal and the Orange Free State, and the British colonies of Natal and the Cape. That this degree of unity should have taken place so soon after the Anglo-Boer War (1899-1902) was remarkable, yet the relationship between Afrikaner and English-speaking South African was to remain brittle for decades. When there was talk of 'the racial problem', it was to this rift in the white community that politicians and journalists referred – a usage that endured right up until after the Second World War.

The slowly simmering issue of rights (or rather, the lack of them) for the great disfranchised majority of the country's citizens was to come to a head only after the accession to power of the Afrikaner-dominated National Party in 1948, when statutory apartheid was gradually implemented. With the prolonged struggle that ensued, South Africa was seen to be a more deeply divided society than ever. Now that this struggle is hopefully coming to an end, the will-o'-the-wisp of true national unity seems at last attainable.

A vast, sun-drenched land

Geographically, South Africa is a sizable country even by African standards (though it is smaller than, for example, Algeria, Libya, Sudan, Zaire or Angola). It extends over an area more than three times the size of California and five times that of the British Isles. It is an irregular lozenge-shaped region girded, in clockwise order, by Namibia, Botswana, Zimbabwe and Mozambique. To the east it almost surrounds one small autonomous state, Swaziland, and it entirely encircles another one, Lesotho. Also within its borders are a patchwork of temporary 'independent' territories (the so-called 'homelands') created by the National Party government as part of its grand apartheid design in the 1970s and 1980s.

To the east and south are the warm waters of the Indian Ocean, to the west lies the chilly Atlantic – a long coastline, nearly 2000 miles in all, and a remarkably regular one, without many pronounced bays, inlets or natural harbours.

In general South Africans enjoy a temperate climate, the average amount of daily sunshine ranging from 7.5 to 9.4 hours (as against, say, London's 3.8). Some of the dust-dry western districts have only ten or so overcast days in a whole year. The interior plateau

An old Afrikaner at his farmstead door. For generations these descendants of the early Dutch settlers have jealously guarded their cultural identity from outside threats, either by trekking away from them or, latterly, by retaining a firm grip on political power. Today, in the new South Africa, Afrikanerdom is having to adapt to the realities of a new order.

mous deposits of cheap coal (58 billion tons of it), asbestos, uranium, nickel and phosphates.

The country's economy employs advanced technologies, its communications are sophisticated and reliable, and commerce, industry and banking are all very highly developed. The litany of assets is impressive: South Africa's foreign trade accounts for 40 per cent of the whole of sub-Saharan Africa's trade with the rest of the world. The country generates 70 per cent of the subcontinent's electricity and transports 76 per cent of its railed goods. South Africans drive 46 per cent of the entire continent's motor vehicles and use 36 per cent of Africa's telephones.

And yet to get things in a global perspective, South Africa's gross national product per capita is only equal to that of Venezuela. Barring massive international aid, therefore, it is with strictly limited financial and managerial resources that the country's pressing problems must be tackled.

An ethnic melting pot

South Africa has a culturally diverse human population of somewhere around 38 million. Black South Africans are in the majority: they number about 28 million, of whom more than a third are urbanised. That proportion, though, is growing by the year as

Road-running is enormously popular in South Africa; these athletes are competing in Cape Town's Argus Biathlon. Premier event on the ultra long-distance calendar is the Comrades Marathon, held over the 55 miles that separate Durban and Pietermaritzburg. Up to 15,000 men and women take part in the race.

is subject to wide climatic variations, with hot summers and cold winters; the eastern seaboard is warm and tropically humid, while the south-western tip of the country enjoys a distinctly Mediterranean-style climate, with copious winter rains. Over the rest of the subcontinent, rain – often accompanied by dramatic electrical storms – falls in summer.

Perennial rivers pass through only a quarter of the country, and even these watercourses are subject to seasonal flow. Only 12 per cent of the land can be cultivated. It is a tribute to the skills of farmers, agronomists and water engineers that almost every major crop (and many minor ones) can be grown – among them wheat, sugar cane, tobacco, deciduous and citrus fruits, and grapes. Huge expanses are also given over to raising livestock.

Lying beneath the South African soil are large reserves of gold, platinum-group metals, iron-ore, high-grade chromium, manganese, vanadium, fluorspar and andalusite, together with diamonds, enor-

hundreds of thousands are lured to the cities by the prospects of jobs and a better way of life. Urban drift, in fact, is probably the single most significant element of the socio-economic spectrum, and it has unfortunately served to undermine the values, traditions and cultural identities of its various ethnic communities.

Nevertheless the African people, especially those living in the country areas, can still be divided by language and custom into a number of distinctive communities or 'nations' – among them the Xhosa, the Zulu and the Swazi, all three of whom belong to the Nguni group; the Sotho (northern and southern) and the Tswana, who are historically linked; and the Venda and the Tsonga. Each of these, in turn, comprises many different sub-groups or clans.

White South Africans account for about a seventh of the total population and they too can be divided according to language and cultural background. The Afrikaners are descendants of the Dutch, who progressively colonised the Cape from the 1650s onwards, and of other immigrant peoples, notably the late-17th-century French Huguenot refugees and the Germans who settled, much later, in the eastern Border areas. Absorption was complete: practically nothing remains to remind one of the Germans, and the French influence can be discerned only in common Afrikaans family names – De Villiers, Le Roux, Du Preez, Fouche, Marais, Malan, Rousseau, Du Toit, Du

Cape Town's 'Coon Carnival', a vibrantly colourful street parade staged by the city's Afro-European community, is held each New Year.

Johannesburg's streets echo to the strident sounds of a Rasta band. The setting is a fleamarket, one of many that flourish in this and other cities. Bands and buskers, hawkers and sidewalk traders are a relatively recent phenomenon, symptom both of a new freedom and of high unemployment.

Plessis – and, faintly, in some of the lovely architecture of the south-western Cape countryside.

High Dutch was the stem from which the Afrikaans language branched, taking on new words and a different shape over three centuries of isolation from the original homeland. Today an Afrikaner and a Hollander can follow each other in conversation, but not all that easily – the difference is akin to that, say, between the languages of a Parisian and a Breton.

Until recently the Afrikaners were a largely rural people, their families large, close-knit, patriarchal, their heritage one of fierce pride in the community, of tough and uncompromising cultural exclusivity, of

unity under threat. And threat there has been, right from the very beginning: of being 'swamped' by the far more numerous African peoples whose lands they took over, of conquest by the colonial British, of impoverishment by exclusion from the urban mainstream. This last is a spectre that still haunts the older generation: not too long ago, during the Great Depression of the 1930s, over 300,000 Afrikaners, approximately a third of the entire community, were classed as 'poor white'.

South Africa is home to just under two million English-speaking white people. Their background, in contrast to the Afrikaner, is colonial rather than pioneer, urban-industrial rather than rural.

The English presence was initially established by the British military occupations of the Cape in 1795 and, more permanently, in 1806. This presence grew stronger over the following decades as successive waves of immigrants arrived on the country's shores. Most significant of these were the 1820 settlers of the troubled eastern frontier region and, around the middle of the 19th century, the colonists of Natal.

Later, in the 1870s and 1880s, the discovery of diamonds around what became the city of Kimberley, and the discovery of gold on the Transvaal's Witwatersrand attracted hordes of English-speaking *uitlanders* (Afrikaans for foreigners) to the northern areas. In much more recent years, further migrations occurred, most notably after the Second World War

These work-hardened folk are among South Africa's three million people of mixed descent, the great majority of whom live on the Cape's south-western seaboard.

and, in the post-colonial era, with the granting of independence to Britain's East and Central African territories. The slow, painful demise of Rhodesia (now Zimbabwe) prompted an especially large influx.

Apart from the English-speaking farmers of the eastern Cape and the sugar cane and fruit growers of Natal, the English speakers of South Africa constitute a largely urban society. Cape Town, Grahamstown, Durban, Pietermaritzburg and Johannesburg are its strongholds and each of these centres has an English-medium university.

Other, much smaller white minorities are those of recent Dutch, Portuguese, Italian, German and Greek extraction. The Portuguese, many of them from the island of Madeira and the former possessions of Angola and Mozambique, number about 75,000. The Jewish community, whose roots lie mainly in central and eastern Europe, makes up around 2.5 per cent of the white population and is prominent in medicine, law, big business and the arts.

Most of the country's 3.3 million mixed-descent people, once classified as 'coloureds', live in the south-western Cape region. Their origins are diverse; many are descendants of slaves brought in from the East and from various parts of Africa during the early years of Dutch settlement, and of unions between white colonists and the indigenous Khoikhoi (Hottentot), and between settler and slave. They include the 200,000-strong so-called 'Cape Malay' community, which has retained its Islamic traditions. The majority of mixed-descent people, however, are Christian. Afrikaans is spoken in most of the homes.

The fourth major ethnic component of South African society are the Indians, of whom there are about a million. The majority of South African Indians live in Natal, where their forefathers settled in the latter half of the last century.

The main centres of population are concentrated around the mines and industries of the north-central interior and along the southern and eastern coastal belts. The country is divided into four provinces,

Beads have been the central feature of Zulu ornamentation for centuries. However, this woman was not averse to introducing a bit of modern novelty into her headdress!

Some 100,000 residents of Cape Town and its surrounds belong to the Islamic faith, most of them descendants of slaves brought in during the 17th and 18th centuries. These 'immigrants' were highly valued for their skills – and for their exotic cuisine, from which such spicy Cape foods as bobotie, bredie and blatjang evolved. With the abolition of slavery in the 1830s many of the newly freed citizens settled on the slopes of Cape Town's Signal Hill, in the picturesque Bo-Kaap, sometimes referred to as the 'Malay Quarter'.

though the number may change as power is devolved to the regions under a new political dispensation. They are the Transvaal, in the north-east; the Cape Province, which covers the southern and western coastal regions together with much of the interior; Natal, in the east; and the Orange Free State, on the high east-central prairie lands.

Cape Town, in the far south-west of the Cape Province, is the 'Mother City' (this is where the first European settlers made their homes, in 1652) and seat of the country's parliament. Pretoria, in the Transvaal, is the administrative capital and Bloemfontein, in the Orange Free State, the judicial capital. Durban, on the eastern seaboard of Natal, is the largest port city but doesn't enjoy capital status, even a provincial one. Nor does Johannesburg, the engine-room of the economic powerhouse known as the Witwatersrand.

The golden triangle

'I have come from the newly discovered goldfields of Kliprivier, especially from a farm owned by a certain Gert Oosthuizen,' wrote George Harrison in an affidavit to the Pretoria Mines Department. 'I have long experience as an Australian gold digger, and I think it is a payable goldfield.'

The affidavit was dated July 24, 1886, a few months after Harrison and his partner George Walker, two out-of-work miners on their way east to the Barberton fields, stumbled on the main reef of the Witwatersrand – the 'ridge of white waters' that was to prove to be the world's most fabulous treasure-house.

News of the find spread like the proverbial bushfire, and the wagons and bivouacs of the fortune-seekers began to spread across the bleak, treeless highveld landscape. Johannesburg – Jo'burg, Joeys, the Golden City, *Egoli* to the Zulus – had been born.

Within three years the place had outstripped Cape Town in size, and it is now the third-largest city on the African continent, a modern, vibrant metropolis of densely packed high-rises and one-way streets jammed with nose-to-tail traffic.

Johannesburg is South Africa's economic capital, the epicentre of a vast, sprawling muddle of mining, industrial and dormitory towns collectively known as the Witwatersrand or simply as 'the Rand' (and sometimes, to confuse things, as 'the Reef'). The conurbation has an inner and outer ring, the former taking in such municipal heavyweights as Roodepoort,

A Hindu ascetic seeks to show that spiritual strength can overcome any physical discomfort. South Africa is home to almost a million people of Indian descent, the great majority of whom live in Natal.

Right, above: Johannesburg is the hub of the giant Pretoria-Witwatersrand-Vaal Triangle conurbation, South Africa's economic heartland. The city was founded on gold: it began life in 1886, when an itinerant Australian digger named George Harrison literally stumbled on the world's richest repository of the prized yellow metal.

Right: Johannesburg's Market Square around the turn of the century. By 1888, just two years after Harrison's momentous discovery, the fledgling city boasted a stock exchange, a racecourse (at Turffontein), school, hospital, the Globe Theatre and the famed Wanderers Club.

A microbiologist at work. South Africa's Indian society is largely regulated by the religions and precepts of an ancient culture, though the old ways are less important to the younger generation, who tend increasingly to use English as their first language, and to observe Western dress, manners and modes.

fashionable Sandton, Randburg, Edenvale, Germiston (a city in its own right and the country's sixth biggest), Alberton, Bedfordview and Soweto, South Africa's most extensive 'black' urban area. Among the outer towns are Westonaria, Carletonville, Randfontein and Krugersdorp in the west; Kempton Park, where the country's main international airport is situated; and Benoni, Springs and Boksburg in the east.

To the south, around the sluggish middle reaches of the Vaal River, is another heavily built-up area, a smoke-hazed heavy-industrial patchwork that embraces the so-called Vaal Triangle. The three points of the triangle are Vereeniging (of Anglo-Boer War treaty fame), the steel town of Vanderbijlpark and, across the river in the Orange Free State, the oil-from-coal complex of Sasolburg.

Pretoria, the conurbation's final component, is 37 miles north of Johannesburg. The two cities are linked by the N1 highway and, increasingly, by the progressive spread of a brand-new metropolis-in-the-making named Midrand.

So much for the broad physical outline. Taken together, Pretoria, the Witwatersrand and the Vaal Triangle, or the PWV area for short, occupies just two-and-a-half per cent of the country's surface but is home to one-fifth of its population and generates around 40 per cent of the national product. Although it is an immensely affluent region, there is also a great deal of poverty in its townships.

Still a mining town at heart

Brash Johannesburg has been described as more of an overgrown mining camp than a city, only a step away from the ruggedly competitive world of the hard-nosed, hard-living, high-spending tycoons of yesteryear. However, for all its go-getting hustle and quest for the quick buck, it has real claims to sophistication, even stylishness, in the way it conducts and enjoys itself. Theatre, music, ballet and opera are of international calibre, the leading restaurants serve exquisite food, the nightspots are exciting, shopping malls glitter, museums and galleries proliferate and thrive and, all in all, the standard of civilised living is borne high.

Nevertheless something of the old digger days remains, discernible in the urgent business pace, and in the endless speculations as to where the gold price is headed, and who is taking over whom. The visual legacy is there too: the early planners weren't overly concerned about public gardens, squares and other such urban amenities and there is still virtually no open space in the central area. Not-so-aged buildings are constantly being pulled down to make way for taller, shinier structures. All in the name of progress and economically justifiable, of course, but in some ways the psychology is still that of a brash, pioneering frontier settlement.

Climb to the fiftieth floor of the Carlton Centre and you'll understand just how pre-eminent the gold in-

The futuristic First National House on Diagonal Street, epicentre of Johannesburg's financial life. Close by is the Stock Exchange.

Until recently, gold was the platform on which the South African economy rested: in the mid-1980s the industry comprised some 60 mines, with a further 16 under development, and a labour force of around 400,000. But the gold price slumped in the early 1990s and many of the more marginal mines were faced with closure.

dustry has been and how commanding it remains. Mine dumps rise from the ground as far as the eye can see, like the burial mounds of some ancient druidical society. The early workings, those close to the city, have long since been mined out and the once-dusty dumps are now decently clothed in coats of greenery, their headgear silent and rusting. But there is much activity in the hugely rich ground further away from the city centre.

The Witwatersrand's Main Reef runs 53 miles from Nigel in the east to Randfontein in the west. This reef forms a small segment of the rim of a gigantic gold-bearing 'saucer' that stretches some 310 miles to a point deep in the Orange Free State. The country's 60-plus mines and some 15 tailings retreatment plants (which squeeze gold from earth excavated during the less-efficient past) employ approximately 400,000 workers to produce 600 or so tons of refined gold each year. The people who go underground live a dirty and sometimes dangerous life. Many of the mines reach enormous depths (nearly two and a half miles at Western Deeps), and in spite of the most stringent safety measures the great pressures under which the ore is extracted can lead to what are known as rockbursts, one of the more common causes of fatalities. Many of the seams are narrow, and the tunnels, or stopes, that burrow into them are little more than three feet high; temperatures are fierce despite the refrigerated air

The inner Johannesburg suburb of Hillbrow is among the southern hemisphere's most densely populated urban areas.

Signs of a new freedom – the entrepreneurial spirit is beginning to flourish in townships long neglected by private enterprise.

Johannesburg's leafier, wealthier suburbs lie to the north of the city; the poorer ones, generally, to the south, though such delineations are becoming increasingly blurred as 'informal settlements' mushroom around South Africa's major centres.

pumped through the networks. The miners are well paid by local standards, and generally well cared for, partly because the companies have traditionally looked after their own and partly because the National Union of Mineworkers has a great deal of muscle.

One of the highlights of a spell in Johannesburg is a mine visit – a morning's tour that also takes in African tribal and 'gumboot' dancing. That will introduce you to the modern scene; shades of a perhaps equally intriguing past can be glimpsed some way south of the city, on the old Crown Mines property, now given over to an evocative re-creation of the early pioneering days of Johannesburg. Gold Reef City is a living museum of Victoriana: its main attractions include an old-style funfair, tea garden, diggers' pub, brewery, cooperage, apothecary, Chinese laundry, newspaper office, stock exchange, steam-train and horse-drawn

omnibus. There's also an array of craft and speciality stores and an elegant four-star hotel *in situ*. Crown Mines, incidentally, has an especially honoured place in the local annals: during its lifetime it yielded the incredible amount of three million pounds of gold, a bounty that would now be worth somewhere around nine billion pounds sterling.

Johannesburg's suburbia is an area of contrasts. The inner areas and those lying to the south are mainly sprawls of modest red-roofed bungalows, unpretentious apartment blocks and commercial streets. On the other hand Hillbrow, just to the north-east of the city centre, does have more bustle and personality: it's a cosmopolitan flatland of high tenements, trendy shops, eateries, discos and streets that seldom sleep.

The northern suburbs are something else again. Here there are dignified, leafy avenues whose stately

nagmaals (Calvinist-type communions, which were highly sociable get-togethers), baptisms and weddings. In the following year the place was renamed Pretoria Philadelphia (Pretoria Brotherhood) in honour of Andries Pretorius, who had defeated the Zulu army at Blood River 17 years before.

In the very early days Pretoria was known as the 'city of roses' because of the luxuriant profusion of ramblers. According to a passing traveller, 'the whole town was drowned, smothered in those fragrant flowers; for each hedge consisted of them, each verandah, each wall was clothed in them'. Later came the town's famous jacarandas, the first two imported from Rio de Janeiro in 1888. About 70,000 of these graceful trees with lilac-coloured blossoms now bring glorious springtime colour to the gardens and avenues.

The 'Jacaranda City', set beneath the heights of Meintjieskop, its eastern suburbs touching the foothills of the Magaliesberg, is South Africa's administrative capital and its corridors teem with dark-suited bureaucrats. It also has its industries, most of them based solidly on the railways, the motor industry and on the giant steelworks established just outside the city. One of the world's biggest diamond mines scours the earth at nearby Cullinan. It was also the capital of the old Transvaal, or more accurately the South African Republic, and it features prominently in the often tragic story of Afrikanerdom. This was Paul Kruger's stamping ground from 1883 until, with Roberts's British columns steadily advancing from the south, he fled to Europe and exile in May 1900. Kruger's residence still stands at the western end of Church Street (which is 16 miles from end to end, making it one of the world's longest urban thoroughfares), a surprisingly modest single-storeyed building.

Pretoria's hub is Church Square, originally designed to imitate (vaguely) Paris's Place de la Concorde on its northern side and Trafalgar Square on its

Pretoria in springtime is a visual feast: September brings the city's 70,000 jacarandas to glorious bloom.

trees shade some of the country's most opulent homes. The wealth of Parktown, Saxonwold and Houghton is discreet, hidden behind quietly decorous facades, but it is real enough, and enormous in its extent and power.

Pretoria – bureaucrats and big business

A half-hour's drive north of Johannesburg lies Pretoria, older than its sister city by some four decades, and generally a lot more attractive. It was founded in the warm and fertile valley of the Apies ('little ape') River when, in 1854, the recently settled Voortrekker farmers of the region proclaimed the village of Elandspoort the *kerkplaas* – namely, the focal point for

southern. It could once have been one of the glories of the continent – a place, if the citizenry of the early 1900s had had its way, of fountains and flowers and Italianate paving, but instead it became a tramway terminus. Still, it has its architectural merits, most notably the Old Raadsaal, or parliament, and the elegant Palace of Justice.

The city's two most striking architectural legacies, though, come from entirely different and in some ways conflicting eras.

Atop Meintjieskop are the Union Buildings – designed by the celebrated British architect Sir Herbert Baker – with their impressive classical Renaissance style. They represent a reconciliation of the two white

tribes, a coming together that was sealed by the creation of the Union of South Africa in 1910.

Four miles to the south is the Voortrekker Monument, completed in 1949 in commemoration of the Boers who fled British rule in the Cape in the late 1830s. It comprises a 130 foot high block ringed by a laager of 64 granite ox-wagons. In one of the two inside chambers, the Hall of Heroes, is a frieze of marble panels depicting the Trek's progress to the promised land. The other chamber holds a granite cenotaph so sited that a ray of sunshine falls on the patriotic inscription at precisely noon on December 16 each year – the anniversary of the Battle of Blood River, when the Boers defeated a 10,000-man Zulu army in what is now Natal.

It is a grand monument, but at the same time, a somewhat unsettling symbol for many people in post-apartheid South Africa.

Soweto – a place of tears and laughter

'Sunny, sullen, scowling, soulful, soulless, swinging . . . pulsating, soccer-crazy, singing, laughing . . . Soweto is all of this and much more.'

This is how a contemporary writer describes the city that straggles across the countryside just to the south-west of Johannesburg – a low-rise, high-density crucible of cultures that squeezes approximately two and a half million people into its dusty confines and which has consistently made the headlines since the watershed students' uprising of 1976.

Soweto, an acronym for SOuth WEstern TOwnships, began as a slum-clearance scheme after the

A purloined supermarket trolley serves as a 'shop on wheels' in one of the country's townships. The so-called 'informal economy' is thriving.

A group of schoolgirls. One of the greatest challenges facing the country is the education of its burgeoning young, and mostly black, population.

Second World War. This was an age of rapid industrialisation with factories and mines drawing tens of thousands of work-seekers to the Rand.

A dozen huge squatter-camps had mushroomed around Johannesburg; the homes within them were described as 'hovels pieced together with scraps of rusty corrugated iron, lengths of hessian, bran and coal bags, boxwood, cardboard and odds and ends ... shin-deep mud in the rainy months, and in winter, incessant screens of blinding dust. Bugs, disease, gangsters ...'.

In order to improve conditions, serviced sites were eventually provided and the homeless encouraged to erect temporary structures until money could be found for permanent housing – which it eventually was, in the later 1950s, through a deal between the Anglo-American Corporation and the Chamber of Mines.

Soweto was always intended to be, and remains, a dormitory town. It has few of the amenities that western city-dwellers take for granted – parks and playgrounds, swimming pools, public libraries, cinemas. There's just one major highway through it, and on either side, stretching to the horizons, are row upon monotonous row of 'matchbox' houses lining mostly unpaved, ill-lit, litter-strewn streets. No high-rises, no glitzy shopping centres breach the skyline. Jabulani (which means 'be happy') is supposed to be the central district but it adds up to little more than a few stores and tenement buildings, a stadium and the local council chambers, and in the daytime it has a deserted, neglected look about it.

A few Sowetans, the especially enterprising or lucky ones, have fine double-storey houses, limousines in the double garages, servants and bodyguards. There is also an emergent black middle class in Soweto, which is growing in size and influence by the year. But by and large, the great majority of Sowetans are poor, living six and more to a room, two to a bed, often with even more people – tenants – crowded into a lean-to at the back. The housing shortage is critical.

The Great (daily) Trek

About 95 per cent of Soweto's working population – the half million or so who have jobs in the formal sector – commute daily to Johannesburg and other Rand centres. The two rail lines operating in and out of Soweto carry 250,000 passengers between four o'clock in the morning of a weekday and eight at night. The trains are cheap, reliable, crowded, dangerous and companionable. There will be *tsotsis* (gangsters), pickpockets and other villains on board, intent on mischief, but the spirit is good: join any tightly packed rush-hour throng on the journey out and you'll hear spontaneous music, clapping and the deep-throated harmony of gospel hymns.

The minibus taxis that fly along the highways to and from Soweto are about twice as expensive as the trains but they offer more comfort, more safety from the *tsotsis* and shorter travelling times. Competition among the owner-drivers is intense because the financial rewards are great. The body that represents the

owner-drivers, the 55,000-member South African Black Taxi Association, is one of the phenomenal success stories of the new entrepreneurial generation: it controls impressive resources, is able to command massive discounts from suppliers, has offered to help improve the transport systems of neighbouring countries and, in the early 1990s, made a bid for the region's government-subsidised but ailing bus corporation.

Sowetans who don't join the daily exodus are the women (those without regular jobs), their children, the elderly – and the unemployed, of whom there are vast numbers. And, too, those who work in the so-called 'informal economy', a euphemism for the thousands of backyard businesses proliferating around the townships of South Africa, partly in response to official encouragement (hawking and street-barter are

Black traditions are being rapidly supplanted by Western ones – especially in and around the big cities. The long-stemmed, wooden tobacco pipe has given way to cigarettes and cigars, and tribal ornamentation, such as bead headbands, earrings and necklaces, are falling away in favour of trendier items.

'Gumboot' and other kinds of mine dancing are popular tourist drawcards in and around the Witwatersrand; performances are given (usually on Sundays) at different venues, among them Gold Reef City, an evocative re-creation of pioneer Johannesburg built on the old Crown Mines site.

Sun City's 15-storey Cascades Hotel offers the ultimate in luxury. Its grounds, 550,000 square feet in extent, have been lavishly landscaped to produce a fantasia of tropical plants and exotic bird life.

capitalism at its purest) and partly as a reflection of the desperate shortage of ordinary jobs.

It is reckoned that the informal sector – a term that encompasses, among other activities, market trading, one-man repair shops, door-to-door vending, *spaza* stores (home shops that stock a limited range at, usually, astronomical prices), crafts such as brick-laying and carpentry and, less legitimately, the *shebeen* trade, prostitution, theft (notably of cars) and drug-dealing – absorbs 2.2 million of the 13 million economically active black people technically classed as unemployed.

Soweto only really comes alive at night and at weekends. The 5000 *shebeens*, taverns and clubs become vibrant with music and dance, and the streets are animated with people – despite the roaming gangs and the criminals lurking in the shadows.

The music of Soweto is something special – there are so many ingredients and origins that it defies any neat classification. The earliest form of township jazz was called *marabi*, a mix of ragtime and the stamping beat of the kraal that, together, produced a bouncy, anything-goes, enormously popular sound. Other, later influences were the American big-band music of Ellington, Basie and Armstrong, the rural *mbube* of the Zulu 'choral bans' (heard at its best in Paul Simon's *Graceland* album), the joyous penny-whistles of Sophiatown and Alexandra, the acrobatic soul-dance music of the 1970s, and the Afro-rock of the 1980s.

A new art form – or perhaps a very ancient one – is also emerging in the world of drama. This is what is termed 'black theatre' – productions that are conceived, written and performed by African artistes largely for African audiences. Some of these reach the more rarified venues of Johannesburg and other South African cities, and a few have been internationally acclaimed. Performers tend to share in the creation of the work rather than follow a set script from the outset.

The privileged pleasures of Sun City

South Africans have long been a nation of frustrated gamblers. Millions are spent on track and tote each year with the blessing of officialdom but, illogically, games of chance that don't involve an element of skill have been strictly forbidden by law.

However, by some quirk of officialdom, gambling was considered legal in the various 'independent' states within South Africa that were created as part of the grand apartheid design as 'homelands' for blacks. Consequently, in 1979 the high-flying South African entrepreneur Sol Kerzner – known locally as the Sun King – built the first of his casino-hotel complexes, Sun City, in a segment of Bophuthatswana, two hours'

drive from the Johannesburg-Pretoria axis. As a result, thousands of respectable citizens began beating a path across the virtually non-existent borders to play the slots and the tables, to take in risqué movies, watch shows of international calibre, eat, drink, and generally have a good time.

Since then several more pleasure-palaces have made their appearance in various 'independent' parts of the country, including an especially attractive one on Transkei's Wild Coast.

But Sun City is still very much the flagship, a glittering extravaganza of hotels (three of them), sumptuous restaurants, bars, shops, theatres, discos and the largest bingo-hall in the world. The 7000-seat Superbowl has hosted the likes of Frank Sinatra and Liza Minelli, and doubles both as a sports stadium (for, among other things, major boxing title fights) and a gigantic banqueting hall.

In the grounds is a 820-yard-long lake carved out of the dry bushveld, and a 'waterscape' of three swimming pools, 12 waterfalls and more than 2100 yards of walkways. A thousand bougainvilleas and a wealth of palms, aloes, euphorbias, coral trees, rare cycads, lawns and flowerbeds grace almost 14 acres of cultivated estate. The golf course was designed by Gary

Player, and the game's top competitors have walked the smooth fairways and greens. The annual Million-Dollar Golf Challenge is one of the world's richest. A second course was recently added.

Latest addition is a 'Lost City' complex, centre-piece of which is the Palace Hotel, a sumptuously ornate affair of columns and curlicues, domes and minarets reminiscent of the Raj at its most eccentric. Its entrance hall rises three storeys; one of its restaurants is set on an island fringed by cascades of water, another is embowered by tropical foliage, and the grounds have their own 3500-tree jungle plus a 110 by 65 yard swimming pool with artificially created, six-foot-high surfing waves.

Kerzner has described the enterprise as 'a fantasy come to life, steeped in the grandeur of old Africa'. The real old Africa, though, never had anything like this. Indeed the contrast between the extravagant frivolity and the poverty of the general surroundings is startling, and uncomfortable – because the people of Bophuthatswana are generally poor, despite the region's potential (it sits on some of the world's largest high-grade platinum-group deposits).

Sun International points out that its investment has been a blessing to the area: Sun City provides work for

The simple cone-on-cylinder hut is home to the majority of Bophuthatswana's rural people. The style, evolved by the Tswana, has largely replaced the 'beehive' in much of South Africa.

nearly 4000 people, most of them local Tswana, and for each person on its staff, there are five others who gain indirect employment; local farmers and suppliers benefit enormously, and some of the money generated in the hotel and its gaming rooms finds its way into new schools, clinics and community services.

Kruger – kingdom of the wild

It's been called the world's biggest zoo, Africa's largest hotel and the prince of parks, and each of these names has some truth in it – especially the last. The Kruger National Park is indeed an aristocrat; it is South Africa's premier wilderness area, occupying a vast tract – nearly 8000 square miles – of primal Africa at the north-eastern corner of the country.

The region is known as the Lowveld, a heat-hazed, low-lying plain that stretches between the high escarpment and the Indian Ocean to the east. In the bone-dry winter months the earth is parched and dusty, the colours are drab, and the perennial rivers reduced to trickles. As a result, the animals congregate around what water there is, presenting a splendid parade for the game-viewer and photographer. But in spring and summer, the season of rains, the countryside is transformed, taking on a rich green luxuriance, bringing the animals back to health and vitality, drawing the migrating flocks of birds.

The Kruger stretches in a long strip from the Crocodile River in the south 217 miles north to the Limpopo. It is big enough to have its regional distinctions: below the Olifants River, which more or less bisects the park, the land is covered by acacia and combretum, marula and bush-willow and, towards the east, by acres of buffalo and red grass shaded by knobthorn trees. To the north of the Olifants the acacia gives way to scrub and woodland mopane, a species whose butterfly-shaped leaves are sweet fodder for the browsers. Landscape and vegetation change yet again in

The Cape eagle owl (Bubo capensis) is one of South Africa's rarer species. Owls are nocturnal birds of prey, seldom seen, but often heard at night. They are easily identified by their specific calls – this one has a deep, vibrant, double hoot.

This strikingly colourful bird is a saddlebill stork, one of the Kruger's more solitary species (though it is sometimes seen in pairs). Saddlebills live in and around rivers and marshes; this one's home is the Luvuvhu River at the far northern, lushly tropical extremity of the Kruger Park. The river, and its neighbour the Limpopo, abound in crocodiles.

the far north, a meeting place of no fewer than nine of Africa's major ecosystems and a remarkable mix of wetland and bushveld, grassy plain and broad lava flat, granite hill and dramatic ravine. Many of the Kruger's 400 different kinds of tree are found in the area, among them mahogany and ebony, ironwood and leadwood, baobabs and groves of ghostly fever trees standing pale and silent in the riverine jungle.

In pure statistical terms the Kruger is in a class of its own, its wildlife more diverse than that of any other game sanctuary on the African continent: the broad sunlit spaces are home to 137 species of mammal and nearly 500 species of bird, among them a splendid array of raptors, 114 different reptiles, 33 amphibians, 227 kinds of butterfly, and 49 fish, including the lung-fish, a 'living fossil' which is thought to be the ancient link between the water and land-based vertebrates.

Of the larger mammals, the impala is by far the most common: about 120,000 graze the savanna plains. These medium-size, reddish-brown antelope are so familiar a sight that after a few hours in the park one tends to ignore them, but in fact they merit a great deal more than a glance: they are graceful animals, and acrobatically spectacular in flight – adults can leap nine feet into the air and, when alarmed, the entire herd will vault and veer in perfect unison, putting on a breath-taking display of synchronised movement.

Other prominent residents are zebra (about 30,000 of them), lordly giraffe, hippo and crocodile in and around the rivers, wildebeest and kudu, sable antelope, reedbuck and the shy waterbuck, eland, tsessebe, the rare roan antelope, warthog, wild dog, and the long-legged cheetah, fastest of all land mammals.

Most visitors, though, are there to see the 'big five' of the wild kingdom – elephant, rhino, buffalo, lion and, least visible of all, the leopard, a solitary, stealthy cat that hunts at night and usually hides during the daylight hours.

The Kruger is also haven to about 7500 elephants, usually gentle creatures that roam throughout the park in herds of 30 or so individuals, though groups of a hundred and more are not uncommon.

Keeping the poachers at bay

Poaching is a problem in the Kruger National Park but far less so than in many other parts of Africa, where some of the elephant populations have been depleted to the point of regional extinction. The international

The bushveld rain-frog's common Afrikaans name translates as 'blow-up', which is precisely what Breviceps adspersus *does when angry or threatened. The species is common enough, but seldom seen: it spends much of its time underground, emerging only at night and after rain.*

Among the Kruger's smaller carnivores is this caracal, a lynx-like cat that hunts by night, stalking prey that ranges from antelope to rodents and lizards. The animal, which has lightning-swift reactions, is capable of catching a bird in flight with a well-timed leap into the air.

*Chacma baboons (*Papio ursinus*) are common in most of the mountainous areas of South Africa. Engagingly human-like, they live in troops of 15 to 100 and spend much of their time foraging for insects, roots and eggs.*

ban on ivory sales, imposed in 1989, was designed to slow if not halt the slaughter. However, although the ban has been welcomed by some conservationists, others have serious reservations about it. The reason for the ban being a contentious issue is that countries such as South Africa and neighbouring Zimbabwe have excelled when it comes to the conservation and management of their elephant populations, so much so that their herds, far from declining, have had to be culled – reduced in size – from time to time. Until 1989, the ivory obtained from culling earned money that found its way back into schemes which helped preserve the subcontinent's priceless natural heritage. That source has now dried up, and the game parks of southern Africa are the poorer for it.

Culling is an unpleasant process, but an ecologically essential one. Elephants are voracious feeders: a single adult will eat up to 650 pounds of grass, leaves and stripped bark in a day, and topple whole trees to get to the tender shoots at the crown. Consequently, a herd tends to leave a swathe of devastation behind it. The resultant effects on the environment can be disastrous, so surplus animals simply have to be removed in order to preserve a proper ecological balance.

Artificial restraints are also placed on the numbers of other species – including hippos and buffalo (the latter numbering about 25,000). By contrast the rhino are cherished. These primeval-looking animals are indigenous to the region but they disappeared long ago, wiped out by overzealous hunters, and it was only in the early 1960s, after a small number were brought in from Zululand, that they re-emerged on the Lowveld scene. These were white rhino, so-called not for their colour (which is dark grey) but for the wide (the Afrikaans word being *wyd*), square-lipped mouth adapted for grazing. Later a number of black rhino, smaller than their cousins, were also reintroduced.

The Kruger National Park lays no claims to exclusivity: its aim is to allow tourists easy and fairly cheap access to the wonders of the country's wildlife legacy. On any given day it will host upwards of 3000 people, many of whom are guests at one or other of the 24 rest-camps. These camps consist of pleasantly shady oases of thatched huts and chalets, linked to each other and to the splendid viewsites, water holes and picnic spots by a 1240-mile network of tarred and good gravel all-weather roadways.

The larger camps, neatly laid out, graced by tall trees, trim lawns and a profusion of flowering plants, offer all the comforts, including a restaurant, a shop that sells groceries and much else. Many of the bungalows are surprisingly spacious, with well-equipped kitchens and airconditioned bedrooms. The biggest camp and headquarters of the Kruger is Skukuza, a self-contained little village.

Although, to many, there may be very little of the classic African safari about Kruger, for the inexpensive family holiday it is probably unrivalled anywhere. Moreover, despite the concentrated human presence, the bushveld remains virtually unspoilt – all the camps, the 'designated areas', the roads and the 'visual bands' that flank them add up to less than three per cent of the area and, as one writer puts it, are 'merely windows looking out on the wilderness'.

The Kruger is only one of a great many public reserves scattered over South Africa's four provinces. Seventeen enjoy national status – they have been proclaimed to protect particular natural environments or particular species: Karoo vegetation, for example, or the lakes and lagoons of the south coast, or the forests and marine life of the Tsitsikamma area, or the bontebok and the mountain zebra.

Safari in style

To the west of the Kruger National Park are some of the world's largest private game sanctuaries and most luxurious private game lodges.

Mala Mala Game Reserve, probably the best known outside the country's borders, offers the ultimate in game-viewing comfort: a lodge done out in expen-

The cheetah is the fastest of all land mammals, able to reach sprint speeds of 62 mph in very short bursts. The Kruger Park's cheetah number a modest 250 or so: predator competition is fierce, and there are relatively few open grassland spaces, which this plains-loving species needs in order to run down its prey.

sive, seemingly rugged 'Out-of-Africa' style; attractive thatched bungalows complete with airconditioning, fitted carpets and his-and-hers bathrooms, superb cuisine and five-star service in countryside that boasts the largest concentration of game in Africa. The rangers are mostly young, mostly charming, knowledgeable and infinitely attentive. Many of the guests jet in from Europe and America for a fleeting taste of the 'real' Africa, and they are pampered from the moment they set foot on the private airstrip.

Other lodges have their own character, distinctions and drawcards. Mbali's 'habi-tents' – canvas-roofed hides built on stilts – overlook the game-rich Nhla-ralumi River and the impression is reminiscent of Kenya's celebrated Tree-Tops Hotel. Tanda Tula, part of the famed Timbavati reserve, is a small complex of thatched chalets from which visitors take game drives ranging over 17,500 acres of fascinating terrain. Sabi Sabi is a large, friendly lodge, known for its sociable evenings in the firelit *boma* (meeting circle protected by a thorny hedge).

Indeed sociability is the keynote of camp life: evening meals are informal, alfresco affairs of good cheer, and they invariably turn into roaring parties; conversation is animated, centring on the ways of the wild, about which the rangers know a great deal, and on the day's viewing score – the types of animal spotted (lion is the prize) and the circumstances of the sightings (here the hunt-and-kill ranks highest).

The routines are fairly standard. Visitors spend much of the day – all but the hottest hours – in a Land-Rover in the company of a ranger-tracker team,

searching the terrain, following spoor. The tracker sits on the bonnet of the vehicle, as one writer puts it, 'like an ebony radar . . . the link between the ranger and the bush'. When there's a contact, the other Land-Rovers – which are linked by radio – home in.

The rangers know that people come to see the large game, and they will do their best to find it, but they must sometimes get tired of looking for the 'big five'

This safari group is from the private and very luxurious Mala Mala lodge, in the game-rich country just to the west of the Kruger Park.

A young Shangaan boy of the eastern Transvaal. Most of the Lowveld's superbly skilled game trackers are Shangaans, a people descended from Nguni stock and thus related to both the Zulu and the Xhosa.

*Widespread throughout the northern regions of southern Africa is the bushveld gerbil (*Tatera leucogaster*), a burrowing rodent that looks, and behaves, somewhat like a miniature kangaroo. Its strong hind legs enable it to perform impressive leaps.*

and of answering the same questions day after day (though you wouldn't know it from their courteous manner). In reality most of them have other, more specialised interests – such as the grasses and trees of the bushveld, the birds, or perhaps the insects. If one steers them around to their own subjects, the talk can be hugely rewarding.

These private game lodges are in business to make money, but to labour the commercial aspects is to do them an injustice. The impetus behind the establishment of many of them has been a genuine desire to conserve and protect the environment and its wildlife, and to try and restore the land to its original condition. The job is a hard and often thankless one, because the bush is under threat from a number of quarters – from land-hungry people, from the proliferation of roads, powerlines and people, from drought, soil erosion, the decline of the water table and the encroachment of alien species.

Harry Kirkman, one-time doyen of the local rangers, recalled that, years ago, 'we used to see thousands of wildebeest trekking from the Kruger Park to the Sabie River here. You could see the dust of the trek from the Drakensberg'. But this no longer occurs. The Kruger's western boundary was fenced off – to stop the spread of foot-and-mouth disease – in the early 1960s and, although the neighbouring private reserves are enormous, the game has been confined to the park, unable to move with the seasons. This has threatened the delicate balance between animal and food resources, and between predator and prey. The fences are now coming down, but a great deal of damage has been done over the past three decades.

It is these challenges that the owners of Londolozi, for instance, have taken up, spending huge amounts of

money on clearing bush, restoring water holes, reintroducing and nurturing the game – the nyala and the sable, the reedbuck and the tsessebe – that had all but disappeared from the area. The tourists who come to stay, and the hunters who pay handsomely for the privilege of culling surplus animals, together help fund this very worthwhile work.

The land of Buchan and Haggard

John Buchan, the well-known British author and teller of stirring tales, spent a memorable time in the wilds of the north-eastern Transvaal. 'Two pictures I have always carried to cheer me in dismal places,' he wrote long afterwards: 'One is of a baking sun on the highveld. The other is the Woodbush . . . You climb to it through bare foothills . . . and enter a garden. The Woodbush itself is the extreme of richness and beauty. The winds blow as clean as in mid-ocean . . . .'

The Woodbush is lovely indeed, a magical highland expanse of redwoods and giant ironwoods, yellowwoods, cabbage trees, red stinkwoods – a place for contemplation, and for communing with the true spirit of the wild.

Below, in the hugely fertile Letaba River valley, is Tzaneen, centre of one of the country's richest farming regions. The area has a tropical feel about it, a quality acquired from its place at the foot of the eastern Transvaal plateau, from the kindly rains and from generous soils that nurture citrus and avocado, mango and banana, litchi and pawpaw, coffee, macadamia and pecan nuts, passion fruit and cotton. Flowering trees decorate the countryside; timber plantations

The lesser bushbaby (Galagomoholi), *found in the north-eastern part of the country, is a delicate little mammal about the size of a squirrel, whose spectacular leaps it can easily match. This nocturnal animal spends most of its time in trees.*

Much of the sub-tropically fertile Letaba area, in the north-eastern Transvaal, is given over to tea. The emerald green plantations stretch to far horizons; the summer air is fragrant with the scent of the fresh leaves.

mantle the hillsides. In addition, great emerald fields of tea stretch to the horizons – and in the long harvesting months from September through to May, the air is wonderfully scented with its aroma.

Some little way to the north of Tzaneen lies the realm of the Modjadji, the mysterious Rain Queen. Another writer, Rider Haggard, based his novel *She* on the legends that wreathed this near-mythical figure. The first Rain Queen is thought to have been a 16th-century princess of the Karangan dynasty of what is now Zimbabwe, who fled south across the Limpopo with her people to found the Lobedu clan. She and her spiritual successors, keepers of the rain magic, were held in awe throughout the subcontinent: even Shaka, the Zulu warrior-king supreme, treated her with cautious respect and as a result the Lobedu were left alone during the genocidal wars of the early 1800s. There apparently still is a Rain Queen – the title is handed down from generation to generation by a complex and mystical process.

Tzaneen is at the northern end of the high, sometimes precipitous range of mountains that marks the division between the central plateau and the low, game-rich plain that rolls away to the Indian Ocean in the east. This is the Transvaal Drakensberg or Great Escarpment, a grand region of soaring peaks and deep ravines, clear mountain streams, entrancing water-

Cutting through the Transvaal's beautiful escarpment countryside is the Long Tom Pass, named after a siege gun used by the Boers in the Anglo-Boer War.

The scenic Horseshoe Falls on the Sabie River. The eastern Transvaal abounds in waterfalls, with names such as Mac-Mac, Bridal Veil, Lisbon and Berlin.

falls, scarlet-flamed aloes and dense forest that for centuries was home to the San (Bushman) and then to the more numerous and more warlike Bantu-speakers.

The Voortrekker pathfinders crossed the range in the late 1830s in quest of a route to the Indian Ocean, an odyssey that ended in tragedy, but their kinsmen persevered and managed to establish a small republic in the hills. Later still, in the 1870s, came the pick-and-shovel prospectors, hardy men with dreams of the golden lode – which they found, so launching the first of the great rushes. Their camps in the high country were at Spitskop and Mac-Mac – so named for the number of Scotsmen who arrived on the scene – and, most notably, at Pilgrim's Rest. This camp quickly developed into a pretty little town of solid houses, a school, a church, stores, canteens and a hotel – the pub of which was transported, lock, stock and barrel, from

The evocative little town of Pilgrim's Rest pioneered the eastern Transvaal's once flourishing but now long gone gold mining industry. Thousands of visitors walk its main street every year for an evocative trip into the pioneering days of the old-time gold-diggers.

The ubiquitous dung-beetles, members of the scarab family, feed on and lay their eggs in dung, which they roll into large balls and move by pushing them along, backwards, with their powerful hind legs.

the coastal centre of Delagoa Bay where it had served, rather more respectably, as a chapel.

Eventually the gold began to run out, but by that time the claims were consolidated and the controlling company had enough money, and enough foresight, to diversify – specifically into timber–and the region now has some of the world's largest man-made forests. As a result, Pilgrim's Rest survived – unlike some of the other gold-inspired ghost towns. Pilgrim's Rest is still a working town, but it is also a living museum, with the early miners' cottages and other buildings beautifully restored to their original and enchanting character. The Royal Hotel and its bar still function in a lively enough fashion, and the rooms you sleep in are as they were a century ago, complete with brass beds.

These uplands offer a plethora of scenic riches, though for sheer spectacle none comes anywhere near the Blyde River Canyon, just to the north of Pilgrim's Rest. Over the millennia the waters have cut through sandstone and dolomite to create a gorge that is more

The picturesque Royal Hotel at Pilgrim's Rest combines the comforts of a modern hostelry with the lively memories of an eastern Transvaal mining town of the 1870s.

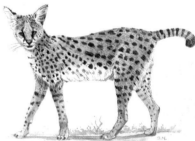

The serval (Felis serval), which looks somewhat like a miniature cheetah – though the latter has proportionately smaller ears – preys on rodents and game birds, and is not averse to raiding farmsteads.

than 2300 feet deep in places, and the views down into the dammed river below are unforgettable.

Far to the south the landscape dips to a series of gentle slopes and then rises again to become the Natal Drakensberg, the highest segment of the Great Escarpment. The mountains are comparatively young, formed about 150 million years ago when seismic convulsions deposited vast quantities of basalt lava onto the sandstone plains, thus creating a plateau 124 miles in length, nearly 9000 feet above sea level.

The plateau is at its loftiest in Lesotho, where it is known as the Maluti Mountains and, less formally, as the Roof of Africa, but the mountains are at their most visually dramatic along the eastern rim, where the cliff faces fall almost sheer to the rolling countryside of the Natal interior. Aeons of rain and wind have eroded the heights, sculpting a gigantic fantasia of gorge and pinnacle, buttress and saw-edge ridge. For the climber, the peaks present a superb challenge; to everyone else, they are breathtaking to behold.

The heights, snow-covered in winter and subject to sudden storms of Olympian proportions, have evocative names, such as Cathedral Peak, The Sentinel, The Bell, The Amphitheatre, Chessmen, Giant's Castle, Organ Pipes, Mushroom Rock, Devil's Tooth, and

One of the great natural wonders of southern Africa is the Blyde River Canyon, a massive sandstone gorge that cuts through the eastern Transvaal Drakensberg. In one section the cliff faces plunge nearly 2000 feet almost sheer to the swiftly flowing waters below. Nearby are Bourke's Luck Potholes (right), a fantasia of pool and sculpted rock named after an early (and, in reality, luckless) prospector called Tom Bourke.

Three Puddings – most of them alluding to physical character, a few to the oddities of local history.

According to some, the section known as Champagne Castle was baptised with this name by two British officers who took a bottle of champagne with them on their climb, found it half empty when they stopped for a breather and, rather than accuse each other, courteously laid the blame on the mountain itself.

Another section, called Mont-aux-Sources, was 'discovered' and named in the early 1830s by a group of French missionaries who trekked across the forbidding terrain from the west. It is indeed a 'mountain of sources'. Seven rivers rise in the area, among them the Tugela, which finds its way to the edge of the aptly named Amphitheatre and then plunges some 2800 feet in a series of tumbling cascades and falls, making it the country's highest waterfall. In the depths of winter its upper section freezes into an enormous, glistening sheet of ice.

Some of the finest of all San rock paintings have survived among the caves and overhangs of the Natal

A Lesotho peasant strums his homemade string instrument on the slopes of the Maluti Mountains – the 'Roof of Africa' – that, along their eastern ramparts, are known as the Natal Drakensberg.

The most striking feature of the Drakensberg's Mont-aux-Sources plateau is the Amphitheatre, a massive, 13,000-feet-wide basalt cliff face. On the left is The Sentinel peak, on the right, the Eastern Buttress.

Drakensberg, most impressively in the high walls of the Ndedema Gorge, where 17 rock shelters and caves hold more than 4000 subjects, 1600 of them in one cave alone. For centuries their creators found sanctuary among the mountains, protected by high cave and cleft from both the elements and the predations of their fellow man. They have long since gone, but something of their spirit remains, enshrined in the pictorial representations of the hunt and the trance-like dance, in the leap of an antelope, or the surge of a buffalo across the stone canvas.

The great interior

If you don't take too many limb-stretching breaks on the way, you can drive from Cape Town to Johannesburg in about 14 hours. The first 60 or so miles meander through the green hills and valleys and rich-looking vineyards of the Cape's winelands but, after breaching the last mountain barrier, the road runs

straight and true towards far horizons, through an immense, heat-blasted countryside of parched grey-brown earth and dwarf scrub.

This is the Great Karoo, a semi-arid region that covers much of the Cape Province and some of the Orange Free State – in all, about 154,500 square miles of the high interior plateau. For the most part the terrain is featureless, broken here and there by ·sills and dykes – rocky outcrops known as koppies – thrust up by aeons-old volcanic action and weathered into stark and strange shapes by the periodic rain storms and

The mountains and foothills of the Drakensberg range are magnificent hiking country, though the higher slopes must be approached with caution – sudden storms of savage proportions can suddenly descend on the unwary, literally out of the blue.

The Drakensberg contains perhaps the most concentrated collection of Bushman paintings in southern Africa. This one can be seen in the Schoongezicht cave, probably one of the last refuges of these ancient people before they died out in the area long ago.

floods. Most striking of these is the well-named Valley of Desolation, an awe-inspiring tumble of craggy peaks overlooking the town of Graaff-Reinet.

The word Karoo comes from the Khoikhoi term for dry, sparse or hard, and indeed the region receives very little rain – just two inches or so falls in the western parts each year, rising to something over 13 inches in the east – and there is practically no surface moisture. Still, underground water is plentiful, and is tapped by wind-powered boreholes (many thousands

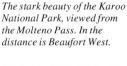

The stark beauty of the Karoo National Park, viewed from the Molteno Pass. In the distance is Beaufort West.

of them) and these, together with the scanty but sweet grasses of the eastern plains, sustain the huge flocks of sheep for which the area is famous.

This vast region is peopled by isolated farmers who own unbelievably extensive spreads, and who have been born to and love the quietness of the great sunlit spaces. The typical Karoo homestead is usually a rambling affair, girded by the greenness of lawn, gumtree and willow, which provide a welcome splash of colour in the monochrome bleakness. The farmer will probably be Afrikaans-speaking, independent of mind, courteous and extraordinarily hospitable. His forefathers pioneered the land and survived its loneliness chiefly because they were resilient people, secure in their large families and their Calvinist faith, but also because they had a wider sense of community, extending a welcome to passers-by because that was the way news was exchanged, goods bought and sold, and the monotony relieved.

Call in at a Karoo farmhouse and the odds are you'll be warmly received, well looked after, and royally fed. The home-cooked meal will be substantial – large portions of good red meat (mutton or venison, or both), sweet potatoes, pumpkin, sweetcorn fritters, mashed vegetables flavoured with cinnamon and nutmeg, milk or custard tart, cheesecake, a selection of *konfyt* (sweet, sticky preserves, crystalised fruits and so forth) and lashings of rich dark coffee. If wine is

The Great Karoo, a vast semi-arid region of scrubby plains, rocky outcrops, low rainfall – and plentiful underground water.

Historic Graaff-Reinet, founded in 1786, is known as the 'Gem of the Karoo' for its neat layout and beautifully preserved old buildings. The Drostdy (magistrate's court) and adjacent cottages, seen here, are now an unusual and charming hotel complex.

The Karoo sustains many of South Africa's nearly three million angora goats, source of fine mohair wool.

served, it will be from the south-western Cape – the heavy, sugary Muscadels being much favoured.

The Karoo's towns are few and far from each other, and from anywhere else. Biggest of them is Beaufort West, situated on the main south-north highway and the first municipality to be proclaimed in South Africa (in 1837). The town is a pleasant place of pear-tree-lined streets and some 26,000 inhabitants. Its most celebrated son is heart surgeon Dr Chris Barnard, whose memorabilia and medals are on display in the local museum.

Farther along the road, almost exactly halfway between Cape Town and the Reef and much used by travellers as an overnight stop, is Colesberg, which is the centre of one of the country's largest horse-breeding areas. Carnarvon, in the remote north, is one of the most isolated of the country's towns, and one of the chilliest on winter nights – a dubious distinction shared with Sutherland, to the south. Outside the latter is part of the national Astronomical Observatory, built here because the skies are clear, pollution-free and unaffected by the obstructive glare of city lights.

These are all modest, rather austere places – undistinguished little farming centres of main street and high-steepled church which few go out of their way to visit. There are, however, two towns of particular interest, both of them situated on the Karoo's southern rim. One of these is Graaff-Reinet, founded in 1786 in a loop of the Sundays River. Popularly termed the 'Gem of the Karoo', the town's early builders were talented craftsmen and more than 200 of the buildings, ranging from simple flat-roofed affairs to gracious Cape Dutch and Victorian mansions, have been restored and proclaimed national monuments.

Even more evocative of long-gone and more elegant times is Matjiesfontein, just off the trunk road some 155 miles from Cape Town. The village was created as a health resort in the 1880s by an enterprising Scot named Jimmy Logan and remains in its pristine

The thunderous cataracts and cascades of the Orange River as it races through the Augrabies Gorge, a name derived from the Koranna word for 'big waters'. The main waterfall is ranked among the world's six largest.

Eland make their way through the bone-dry sands of the Kalahari Gemsbok National Park, a 4000-square-mile wedge of parched northern Cape territory between the borders of Namibia and Botswana.

Victorian condition, right down to the street-lamps, which were imported from London. Its hotel, the proudly turreted and grandly ornate Lord Milner, is just as it was when it hosted the likes of Cecil Rhodes, Lord Randolph Churchill and the Sultan of Zanzibar.

The far western regions of the interior are the most desolate. This is the land of *vloers*, enormous shallow depressions in the arid and gently undulating wastelands that fill with water during the rare rains, and are then leached dry by evaporation, leaving a hard, whitish sediment of mineral salts that reflect the sunlight. These salt pans are blindingly white, the oven-like air above them full of shimmering mirages and dancing dust-devils. Grootvloer, measuring approximately 40 by 25 miles, is the largest; Verneukpan, whose name means 'deception', the most notable.

An unwelcoming and empty region: there's naught here for the comfort of man, but Verneukpan had its brief moment in the headlines when Sir Malcolm Campbell chose it as the venue for his attempt on the world land speed record in 1929. The project was beset by bad weather conditions and by the time he got his vehicle *Bluebird* onto the flats, Henry Segrave had gone even faster, setting Campbell a target he couldn't hope to achieve. But he went ahead anyway, besting the five-mile and five-kilometre marks.

Farther north is Gordonia, South Africa's largest magisterial district, 20,850 square miles in extent, consisting mostly of a flattish wilderness of scrub and, towards the borders of Namibia and Botswana, endless expanses of red Kalahari sand. But it has its surprises: Upington, the principal town, is refreshingly attractive; the irrigated lands around the Orange River are palm-graced, fertile, even lush, and the local gemstones are both beautiful and easily found.

Travel about 100 miles to the south-west of Upington and you'll find the Roaring Sands, a huge 'island' of white dunes that derive their name from the eerie moaning sound, rising to a muted roar, which they emit when even slightly disturbed. Out of town, about 75 miles to the west, is the Augrabies Gorge, a massive ravine through which the Orange River races in a spectacular series of rapids and cascades. The granite formations here are immensely ancient, the rock dating to three billion years ago; 19 separate sheets of water drop from the rim of the main canyon to the deep pool 300 feet below. The Augrabies ranks among the world's six largest waterfalls; in unusually wet seasons upstream, and when in full flood, the flow exceeds 90 million gallons a minute, which compares well with that of the Zambezi's much more famous Victoria Falls.

The common duiker (Sylvicapra grimmia) is a widely distributed little antelope. The name is derived from the Afrikaans word for 'to dive', a reference to the way it plunges into the undergrowth when disturbed.

The Augrabies Falls National Park, established in the 1960s to conserve the landscape on both sides of the Orange River, was recently enlarged with the addition of a 173,000-acre home for black rhino and other game.

South Africa's rail network changed over to electricity and diesel comparatively recently: steam trains, most of them tourist showpieces, attract enthusiastic hobbyists from all over the world.

The 'boer goat', a hardy domestic animal prized by the rural peasant communities of the north-western Cape and the various 'homelands'. There are wide variations in appearance and coloration within the stock, though an 'improved' strain is being bred for its meat.

Romantic refugees from the age of steam

The train – a 1938 Class 19D locomotive and eight exquisitely restored vintage coaches – pulls out of Pretoria station in the warmth of a summer's day on the first leg of its 620-mile journey. It will puff its venerable way past the coal-mining town of Witbank and then through pretty little villages set among the spectacular mountains and dense pine plantations of the eastern Transvaal escarpment. There will be pleasant digressions en route: a visit to the historic mining village of Pilgrim's Rest; a night at one of the luxurious private game lodges in the hot lowveld down below; a few hours guided viewing around some of Africa's finest big-game country.

The trip – known as the Rovos Rail steam safari – lasts four days, and along the way the 30 or so passengers on board (some of them steam-buffs who have flown in from far places for the trip) enjoy *cordon bleu* cuisine and five-star service in an opulent, time-honoured setting. One of the coaches was built by the Metropolitan Carriage and Wagon Finance Company in Birmingham, arriving in South Africa in 1919, and its best suite has twin beds, richly panelled walls, a private bathroom and a plushly fitted out little sitting room.

The dining car dates from 1924, though carved-timber roof supports and arches give it a rather charming Victorian look. Some of the guests dress formally for dinner. The observation car, also from the 1920s, has a glassed-in section at one end, a well-stocked bar

at the other and comfortable armchairs in between. At various stages of the journey other locomotives will take over – perhaps an 1893 Class 6 ('Tiffany') or a 1926 Class 15.

The Rovos Rail steam safari is just one of the more recent ventures into reviving South Africa's age of steam – which was only very recently eclipsed by diesel and electricity. The country's rail system was in fact among the last in the industrialised world to change over to diesel and electricity, since massive and cheap coal resources enabled the old ways of locomotion to remain viable. Commercial steam trains were still running in the Cape in the late 1970s, and some of the grand old work-horses have been rescued from their graveyards around the country.

However, by the early 1990s nostalgia-addicts had an enticing selection of trains and routes from which to choose. Scheduled runs are made by, among others, the dinky little Apple Express (from Port Elizabeth towards the green and pleasant Long Kloof) and the Outeniqua Choo-Tjoe (between Knysna and George in the southern Cape), both of which are long-service working trains that only incidentally take on passengers. Others include the Natal south coast's Banana Express, the irregular steam run between Kimberley

and De Aar in the depths of the Karoo, and a growing number of sporadic services and specially laid-on excursions – from Johannesburg west to the Magaliesberg, for example, and from Cape Town into and around the lovely winelands.

The attractions of rail aren't confined to steam, though. The ultimate in luxury travel is the Blue Train (in fact, two identical 16-coach trains, each pulled by two electric locomotives) that makes the 1000-mile run between Pretoria-Johannesburg and Cape Town. Lounge, dining car and compartments are beautifully appointed, the food superb, the service impeccable.

Other long-established 'name' trains, each with its own personality, are the Orange Express (or Trans-Oranje), the Drakensberg Express, the Trans-Karoo Express and the Diamond Express (which makes an overnight run from Kimberley to Pretoria; among its many luxury touches is a telephone in each of the compartments).

These trains belong in spirit to a more leisurely age, so when it comes to speed they're not in the same league as the city-to-city and trans-continental bullets of Europe and North America. Still, they have their charm, their own brands of comfort, and they are a marvellous way of seeing this vast country.

The scenically enchanting Longkloof region, through which the Apple Express passes. The plant life, seen in the foreground, is typical mountain 'fynbos', a hugely varied vegetation type peculiar to the south-western and southern Cape. This botanical region, despite its tiny extent, is classed as one of the world's six floral kingdoms.

The 'Outeniqua Choo-Tjoe', a working steam train that also carries passengers, negotiates the Kaaimans River mouth on its way from George to Knysna in the southern Cape. Knysna and the neighbouring Wilderness area are known for the chain of lovely lagoons that fringe the coastline.

A typical Sotho homestead in the eastern Orange Free State. The wall decorations are created by the women of the family.

Exploring the Orange by inflatable craft. The river is by far the country's largest watercourse, rising in the high Maluti Mountains in the east to flow westwards before discharging into the Atlantic Ocean on South Africa's border with Namibia.

become what one visitor described at the turn of the century as 'one of the neatest and, in a modest way, best appointed capitals in the world. Gardens are planted with trees that are now so tall as to make the whole place swim in green'.

The description is still apt enough, though of course the city is now much larger, its growth galvanised by the exploitation of the super-wealthy Orange Free State goldfields centred around Welkom, 95 miles to the north-east, and by the giant Orange River Project, which was launched in the early 1960s.

The Orange, by far and away South Africa's largest river – it drains roughly half the entire great central plateau – rises in the Maluti Mountains of Lesotho in the east and flows westward, gathering volume on its

A large land with small beginnings

Bloemfontein, capital of the Orange Free State and judicial capital of South Africa, lies on the high central plateau between the Orange and the Vaal rivers, a quiet, small city of handsome civic buildings, museums and solid monuments recalling a past rich in character and event.

The city was founded in the 1840s as the residence and office of the British agent in the no-man's-land region of Trans-Orangia; he bought the property for £37 and 10 shillings. Bloemfontein became the capital of the Orange Free State in 1854, and grew slowly to

More than half of South Africa's sheep are merinos (right), introduced in the late 1700s and now bred for both their fine wool and their meat. Around 80 per cent of the national flock is nurtured on the broad grassland plains of the Orange Free State.

1450-mile journey to the Atlantic Ocean. It's an erratic river, its character shaped by the seasonal rains: at times it is sluggish, at others a broad, swift-moving torrent. The waters have been extensively harnessed and large expanses of land along its middle and lower reaches, together with the soil-rich islands (once the haunt of river-pirates and rustlers), have been transformed into wide swathes of lucerne and cotton, fruit plantations, fine crops of dates, raisins and sultanas.

Altogether, the Orange River Project accumulates an annual 1650 million gallons of water to provide irrigation for some 570,000 acres of the Orange River valley and, through a system of canals and underground conduits (one, driven through an entire mountain range, is just over 51 miles long – the world's largest continuous water tunnel), for another 150,000 acres of the eastern Cape. Largest of its dams is the Hendrik Verwoerd Dam in the southern Orange Free State, a 144-square-mile reservoir fringed by holiday resorts and nature reserves, one of which is home to huge numbers of the graceful springbok.

The great prairielands of the south and west are for the most part dry, windswept, bare of trees and indeed of any distinctive features, but the soils are good and the grasses sweet, sustaining herds of plump cattle and most of South Africa's 27.5 million head of sheep.

Towards the north, in country drained by the Vaal River, are magnificent fields of wheat and maize, groundnuts and bright yellow sunflowers. In striking visual contrast is the countryside to the east, terrain that rises in a dramatic series of sculpted rock formations, many of them steep-sided and flat-topped, all of them vividly coloured: here sandstone, mudstone,

shale and siltstone combine to paint a quite remarkable canvas of unforgettable golden browns and reds, oranges and yellows.

Part of the region, that especially spectacular portion that lies in the valley of the Caledon River and beneath the high mountains of Lesotho, has been set aside as the Golden Gate National Park. This is primarily a scenic reserve but visitors can also see zebra and antelope and some splendid birds of prey – including the lammergeyer, or bearded vulture.

Mushroom Rock, one of the more prominent sandstone formations in the Orange Free State's magnificent Golden Gate Highlands National Park.

The green and pleasant countryside around Ficksburg, in the eastern Orange Free State. The land here is especially fertile, including in its bounty grain and corn, peaches, apricots, plums, the largest cherry orchards in southern Africa, and wide, rich pastures that sustain great numbers of sheep and cattle.

Kimberley's original mine was initially known as Colesberg Kopje, a diamond-rich hillock that soon vanished as the diggers worked their way ever deeper into the 'blue ground' of a giant kimberlite pipe . The mine closed in 1914, by which time the hole – until recently ranked as the world's largest man-made crater – had yielded over three tons of diamonds. Half filled with water, the Big Hole now forms the main attraction at the Kimberley mine museum.

Glittering wealth beneath the ground

The Big Hole, a gaping open-cast mine dug mainly by pick and shovel, plunges more than 700 feet into Kimberley's volcanic ground. It marks the site of the area's original diamond diggings and, in its day – when it was more than 2500 feet deep – it was one of the wonders of the mining world. At one time about 30,000 men beavered away cheek-by-jowl in its Stygian depths in quest of instant fortune, and by the time it closed down in 1914 it had yielded more than three tons of diamonds.

Today, erosion of the sides has reduced the hole to less than a third of its original depth, and this is now partially filled with water. It now stands as the centre-piece of the Kimberley Mine Museum, which in-cludes a re-creation of part of the old town – complete with cobbled streets, Victorian shops, miners' cot-tages and a diggers' pub. An authentically recon-structed tram with overhead lines runs back and forth between the mine museum at the Big Hole and the centre of the city. The museum also features other vintage rail and road vehicles, early headgear and dis-plays of diamonds, including a copy of the renowned 'Eureka'. Way back in 1866 15-year-old Erasmus Jacobs spotted a 'pretty white pebble' on the banks of the Orange River near Hopetown. A neighbouring farmer, Schalk van Niekerk, arranged to have it exam-ined and it was dispatched to a Dr William Atherstone of Grahamstown in the eastern Cape, who pronounced it a 21,25 carat gem valued at £500.

Oddly enough, the discovery of the 'Eureka' caused hardly a stir and it was only when, three years later, Van Niekerk produced another stone – which he had bought from a local shepherd for the princely price of ten oxen, 500 sheep and a horse – that the headlong rush began. The diamond, later to be known as 'The

Star of South Africa', weighed nearly 84 carats and, predicted the Cape colonial secretary of the time, was 'the rock on which the future success of South Africa will be built . . .'.

Prophetic words indeed. The find attracted international attention, and by the end of 1869 over 10,000 claims had been pegged along the Vaal River.

These alluvial workings were simply the aperitif before the glittering banquet. Not long afterwards five diamondiferous 'pipes' were discovered well to the south, four of them in an area that included the farms Bultfontein and Vooruitzicht. The latter was owned by the De Beer brothers, and among its rocky hills was Colesberg Kopje, the 'cap' of what, after the first of its stones was accidentally unearthed in July 1871, was to prove to be the biggest treasure-house of all. Within a year 50,000 men had congregated in an unruly tent-town that straggled across the veld.

Kimberley is now a respectable little city that still produces diamonds (four of the pipes remain productive) but also serves as a centre for the region's cattle ranches and irrigated farmlands. A great deal of the rugged past remains, its form if not its spirit captured in the museum and by the pleasant period homes that have survived, and by the diamond dealers who trade in town. Hints of a less restrictive, more lively era are conveyed, too, by Kimberley's two drive-in pubs – the only ones to be found anywhere in the world.

South Africa is one of the world's leading suppliers of gem diamonds, producing about 10 million carats a year through operations controlled, largely, by the De Beers organisation. The Kimberley workings rank among the country's larger mines, but it is not the largest – this honour goes to the Premier mine near Pretoria, which is the world's second-largest diamond-producing mine. The Premier mine was the site of the most famous of all diamonds – the Cullinan Diamond. This 3106-carat diamond was discovered in 1905 and was subsequently presented to King Edward VIII in 1907. It was then cut into 96 brilliants, seven

gems and two of the best-known jewels of the Royal regalia – 'The Star of Africa', set in the royal sceptre, and 'The Lesser Star of Africa', which adorns the Imperial crown.

Alluvial diamonds are still found in the inland gravels of the Vaal, lower Orange and Harts rivers and in some of the ancient, now-dry watercourses of the northern interior. The most dramatic of this century's discoveries – and the last and perhaps wildest of the great rushes – occurred near the small far-western Transvaal town of Lichtenburg, on the farm Elandsputte, where a sizeable diamond was found in 1926. People poured in from the cities and the depressed country areas to work the ground and to throng the starting lines of the officially organised claim-pegging races: almost 30,000 men and women would take part in a single, frenzied scramble.

Much larger are the private and State-controlled alluvial fields of the arid western seaboard, forbidden to casual tourists (though you may enter with a permit). The deposits north of the Orange River mouth, in today's Namibia, have been exploited since 1908 but, although the potential of the estuary itself and of the desolate terrain to the south had long been suspected, it wasn't until 1926 that the first major find was made, by Jack Carstens, a young Indian Army officer home on leave.

Once again prospectors converged from all parts to try their luck, and some enjoyed richer pickings than they could ever have imagined. One – the celebrated

The Kimberley mine museum – which embraces the Big Hole together with the original diggings and restored buildings – gives visitors an authentic taste of the town as it was in its flamboyant heyday.

Rough stones from the fabulous fields. South Africa is one of the world's leading suppliers of gem diamonds; the industry is controlled by the giant De Beers group.

A familiar sight along South Africa's shores is the common tern (Sterna hirundo) which, except for its black wing-tips and grey rump, is very similar in appearance to its Arctic cousin. The birds follow the sun: they breed in the northern hemisphere and then migrate, arriving in South Africa for the southern summer.

The 10-mile-long Langebaan Lagoon, on the Cape's west coast, is both a playground for water sportsmen and the focal point of a magnificent natural wetland.

In springtime, daisies (right) and other wild flowers bring glorious colour to an otherwise bleak countryside.

The cushion star (Patriella exigua), although brilliantly hued, is often hard to spot: the colours resemble those of its watery surrounds, and disguise the starfish's outline.

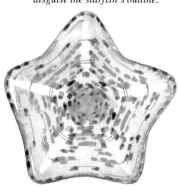

geologist Hans Merensky – retrieved 487 diamonds from beneath a single rock and, during a 30-day period, collected a record 2762 precious stones.

In some areas the luck was reinforced by a curious natural phenomenon: the diamonds occurred in gravels containing fossils of an extinct species of oyster. The two elements – shellfish and gemstones – have nothing in common, but they were connected by some geological phenomenon that had changed the ocean currents, killing the oysters and sweeping the diamonds ashore. The presence of large numbers of fossilised oyster shells thus served as a beacon to the fabulous wealth of the desert dunes.

Seas and shores

Langebaan Lagoon, on South Africa's west coast, is one of the world's great wildfowl preserves, its clear, shallow waters and rocky islands acting as a magnet for vast numbers of cormorants and flamingoes, herons, gannets, turnstones, sanderlings, gulls and ibis.

In the hot summer months there are about 5500 individual birds in residence, a high percentage of them curlew sandpipers and other migrants that leave their Arctic and sub-Arctic breeding grounds for the long and often final flight to the sunny south.

For all its busy bird life though, Langebaan is set at the lower end of one of the bleaker parts of the subcontinent – a treeless and largely featureless, sparsely populated, dry country. Most of the coastal strip that stretches up to the diamond-rich Orange River mouth in the far north is termed 'sandveld', a strange, barren-

looking region of rocky, windblown shorelines backed by raised beaches – the legacy of a time when the sea was about 300 feet or so higher than it is today.

Surface water is almost non-existent in the sandveld, and the ground-cover thin, comprising for the most part scatters of dwarf vegetation. What moisture there is comes from the dense mists that sometimes roll in from the Atlantic Ocean at night, and from the meagre rainfall which, towards the north, amounts to a token two inches a year.

Yet the region, much of which appears on the maps as Namaqualand, is famed for its brief but quite magnificent profusion of wild flowers: about 4000 different species in all, most of them members of the

The worker on the right is from Wuppertal, a picturesque village inland from the Cape's west coast. The settlement – a charming cluster of limewashed, dark-thatched cottages – was founded as a mission station in 1830 and has remained virtually unchanged since then. The area is renowned for its tobacco, its rooibos (red bush) tea, and for its springtime carpets of wild flowers (below).

In contrast to that of other waterbirds, the plumage of the cormorant is not waterproof, and as a result the bird quickly loses body heat when diving for fish. To restore warmth it will rest with its wings spread out – as if holding them out to dry, but in reality exposing the short down of its back to the sun. This is the widely distributed white-breasted variety, Phalacrocorax carbo.

daisy and mesembryanthemum families, though there are many others – aloes, lilies and perennial herbs.

The plants are resistant to drought, and their seeds lie dormant for long periods of time, but after the winter rains, and just before the onset of the desert winds, they sense a warming of the earth and the imminent arrival of the pollinators, and, in a matter of days, they burst into life to cover the countryside in glorious carpets of colour.

Until recently South Africa had a flourishing fishing industry, but over-exploitation and inroads made by foreign fleets have drastically depleted the marine resources. Still, the catches – Cape hake, kingklip, tuna, snoek, monkfish, mackerel and the pelagic round herring, pilchard and anchovy – remain reasonably rewarding. Most of the national catch is taken off the west coast where the upwelling of the cool water carried in the Benguela current creates ideal conditions for nutrient-rich plankton, the food of the pelagic fish which, in turn, sustain larger species.

Most of the trawlers operate out of Cape Town and Saldanha Bay, the latter being one of the few really good natural harbours along the country's entire 1836-mile coastline. Saldanha could in fact have been chosen as the site of the first European settlement, but the area is bone-dry and the early navigators passed it by in favour of well-watered Table Bay, 68 miles to the south. Saldanha, though, has begun to fulfil its promise: it's been developed into a terminal capable of taking the largest of bulk carrier vessels and is linked by an electrified 535-mile railway to Sishen in the northern Cape, around which about half of South Africa's 10 billion tons of iron ore is located.

Altogether different in character is the country's south coast, which extends from Cape Hangklip (situated at False Bay's eastern corner) to Cape Padrone (a point to the east of Port Elizabeth). Running along its entire length, and perhaps the most striking segment of South Africa's entire marginal zone, is a series of splendid upland ranges collectively known as the Cape Fold Mountains. Nowhere do these ranges – the Langeberg, the Outeniqua, the Tsitsikamma and the Swartberg among others – quite touch the shoreline,

A fisherman of Hout Bay, an enchanting little town on the Peninsula south of Cape Town. In June and July huge quantities of snoek are caught offshore and sold directly on the quayside.

The pear limpet encrusts seaside rocks from Cape Town's Table Bay eastwards to the town of Port Edward in Natal.

Cape gannets (rear) and jackass penguins on Malgas Island, off the Cape south coast. The latter are so named for their loud, braying call.

so there are few massive promontories. Uplands and ocean are separated by a narrow, lush plain rich in flora and of extraordinary beauty.

Especially lovely is the 143-mile stretch from Mossel Bay to Storms River, a strip known as the Garden Route. On one side is the shoreline's kaleidoscope of bays and coves and golden beaches, cliffs, lagoons and navigable river estuaries; on the other, the heavily wooded slopes of the Outeniqua hills. In between lies the coastal terrace, the so-called 'garden'.

The highlands receive a healthy 100 inches of rainfall a year and the rains are gentle and perennial, nourishing the region's clear streams, the dense acres of evergreen trees and the multiplicity of its plants. A visiting Frenchman, Francois le Valliant, wrote in the 1780s: 'The earth is covered with flowers, whose mingled perfumes delight the smell, and invite you to loiter in this charming spot, where every beauty that imagination ever gave to fairyland seems realised.'

South Africa's east coast, extending about 630 miles from Cape Padrone to the Mozambique border, falls into two distinct regions. The first and by far the longest stretch takes you up to the Mhaluzi River just to the south of the fast-growing port of Richards Bay. It's a remarkably straight shoreline (Durban's Bluff is the most prominent irregularity) though far from featureless. Indeed its wide, rock and lagoon-flanked golden beaches, its plant life (which becomes lusher the farther north you travel), the beauty of the hinterland, and the bright warmth of its days combine to create one of the handsomest of the southern hemisphere's seaboards.

Especially attractive is Transkei's Wild Coast, an unspoilt wilderness of cliffs and reefs that poke finger-like into the sea, of lonely bays backed by dune

woodlands and rounded hills. The land is green and moist: many sparkling rivers find their convoluted way from the uplands into the warm waters of the Indian Ocean. A magnificent coast – but also a treacherous one, being the graveyard of scores of ships since the first Portuguese set their sails for the Indies. The wrecks are now a perennial lure for divers in search of coins, jewellery, gold, silver and artefacts.

Some of South Africa's most popular holiday resorts are strung out along the shoreline farther north,

Leisure time on the Keurbooms River, one of several navigable waterways on the Cape south coast, and a great favourite with holidaymakers.

The Wild Coast. Transkei's 200-mile Indian Ocean shoreline is an unspoilt wilderness famed for its scenic beauty. and notorious for its dangerous seas.

between the Transkei border and Durban. Liveliest is probably Margate, named after and rather like the English seaside town – it has superb beaches and all the standard amenities, but also an uninhibited *joie de vivre* that lifts it above the ordinary.

The Dolphin Coast north of Durban is similar in character but the resorts are not as numerous and the scenery (and climate) is more tropical, the shoreline graced by lala palms and hibiscus, Madagascar casuarinas, bougainvilleas and other strikingly colourful trees and shrubs.

Finally there's the Zululand stretch, which forms the southern portion of the Mozambique coastal plain. Here the backing dunes are high – over 400 feet in places – though the general region tends to be flat, a sandy, bushy country with a sticky, hot climate. Inland, though, there are great rolling hills that are cooled by the uprising sea air and kept green by the mists and drenching rains.

The glittering mile, and a small corner of India

Hot summers and warm winters have made the Indian Ocean city of Durban one of southern Africa's leading holiday resorts, described by traveller and author H V Morton as having 'an air of musical comedy . . . The light is just a little too strong and white to be sunlight, the flowers are a little too bright to be real, the flamboyant trees seem too exotic to be genuine . . .'.

Durban has served as a premier holiday playground ever since the first land-locked Johannesburgers began coming south in the last decades of the 19th century in search of sun, sea and sand. Its surf and its beaches, packed with bronzed bodies in the long, humid summer months, are world famous. Behind the beachfront is the newly developed and still-growing 'Golden Mile', a lively strip of more than five miles that contains just about everything the heart of the hedonist could wish for.

The Golden Mile is well named: it really does glitter. Here, some of the most elegant of hotels – the Maharani, the Tropicana, the Elangeni among others – rub shoulders with amusement parks, round-the-clock nightspots, glitzy entertainment centres and emporiums, pavilions, playgrounds, piers, an aerial cableway and pools. A place where, as the local television advertisement claims, 'the fun never sets'. For all that, though, its architects have kept good taste firmly to the fore, incorporating into the grand design graceful fountains, walkways, emerald-green lawns and much else of beauty.

This, South Africa's foremost sea port (in terms of general cargo handled) and third-largest city, was born and grew up around a vast, almost entirely enclosed natural harbour that the Portuguese navigator Vasco da Gama first saw on Christmas Day of 1497.

'Rubber ducks' – inflatable boats – prepare to launch into the warm waters of the Indian Ocean from the beach in front of Durban's so-called 'Golden Mile' of hotels, resorts, highrises and restaurants. Millions of visitors flock to these beaches annually – particularly over the traditional Christmas holiday period. Despite the rising popularity of Cape Town, Durban remains the number one holiday resort.

Rickshaws were introduced from the East to Natal in the 1890s, and at first were plain-looking enough, but with competition for tourist fares they and their pullers became elaborately decorative. At one time more than a thousand plied Durban's streets; today fewer than 20 remain.

Durban's Grey Street mosque.

Durban's golden beaches provide summertime fun in the sun for tens of thousands of holidaymakers, most of them visitors from landlocked Transvaal.

Thinking it was a great estuarine lagoon, he named it Rio de Natal ('River of Nativity' or 'Christmas River'). Over three centuries went by, though, before white colonists – Britons – attempted to establish a foothold on what had, in the meantime, become a fiefdom of Shaka's Zulu empire.

The settlement, set uncomfortably on the humid shores of the bay among the mangroves and marshlands, was painfully slow to grow, but began to expand rapidly after the mid-century influx of what were known as the Byrne immigrants – almost 5000 people brought out from Europe by an enterprising Irishman of that name. Jetties and warehouses made their appearance along the dunes of the bay's Point, and the

Durban's Indian heritage has given the city one of its major tourist assets: the feel and flavour of eastern markets. This is the Madressa Arcade, where shopkeepers of Indian extraction sell everything from kerosene lamps to curry powder – including a particularly powerful conconction known appropriately as 'mother-in-law's revenge'.

town itself developed on the firm and level ground beneath the high ridge of hills called the Berea (the name was taken from the Berea of biblical Macedonia, whose people listened to St Paul 'with all readiness of mind', and reflected early missionary optimism).

At the top of the ridge is a campus of the University of Natal, and from the heights here one can take in the whole sweep of city, suburb and conjoining town. It can be seen stretching along the lovely coasts to north and south, and inland to the cool and misty upland plateau where, free from the worst of the summer's heat, some of the more wealthy suburbs are to be found.

The city itself is modern, handsome, its tall buildings densely packed together and gleaming white in the strong sunshine, the enormous size of its central blocks a legacy of the injunction to its first town planner to lay out unusually spacious 'allotments'.

Just to the south is Victoria Embankment, a pleasant thoroughfare that lines one of the hemisphere's biggest and busiest harbours: it has around 17,500 yards of quayage for commercial shipping, its elevator can process grain at the rate of some 1300 tons an

hour, and it is specially equipped to handle coal and anthracite, manganese ore, oil and sugar. About 30 million tons of cargo pass through the port each year.

Greater Durban is home to large numbers of people of Indian extraction, many descended from the indentured labourers brought in during the decades after 1860 to work the sugar plantations of the hinterland. They were contracted for a period of three years, followed by five years as 'free' workers. They then had the choice either of repatriation, or the grant of a small patch of Crown land. Most chose the latter, and they were joined by thousands of their compatriots, ordinary immigrants (called 'passenger Indians') who, as British subjects, could travel more or less freely within the Empire.

The majority of the newcomers were from the Tamil and Telugu-speaking Madras area, but the

Right: sari-clad Indian women bring grace and colour to Durban's public places. The community's most famous son was Mohandas Gandhi, architect of modern India, who waged a 20-year battle for civil rights before his departure in 1914.

Children dressed up in their finery for the candle-lit Deepavali festival. Some of the ancient traditions are disappearing, but the pull of Mother India is still strong.

growing community also attracted numbers of traders from the state of Gujarat. It was to protect the interests of these people – hard-working businessmen whose success earned them the hostility of whites – that a young lawyer named Mohandas Gandhi came to Durban in 1893. He stayed for over 20 years.

Take a short walk away from Durban's central blocks and you'll find yourself in a small corner of India, an animated, marvellously exotic world of saris and fine-boned, graceful women, of pungent scents of spices and incense, sandalwood and rose, of sounds of haunting melodies and the languages of Bombay and Calcutta. The shops are crammed to their lowest shelves with satins and sumptuous silks, ceramics, exquisite jewellery, baubles and beads, silver, bronze and acres of brass, craftware, aromatic foods, shirts, shoes and endless bargains. In Grey Street stands the southern hemisphere's largest mosque, an impressive edifice of golden domes that catch the evening light.

Around half of South Africa's one million Indians live in and around the Durban-Pinetown-Verulam conurbation, and it is a generally prosperous, remarkably homogenous community that has retained its distinctive customs and beliefs. Relationships are underpinned by the kutum, the patriarchal extended family, and by religion – Muslim and Hindu. The former speak Gujarati and Urdu, the latter Gurarati, Hindi, Tamil and Telugu. Many of the less fundamental traditions, though, are being eroded, especially among the younger people: the trend is away from the larger family unit, the women live freer lives than they used to, and English is now the common language.

Durbanites of European descent also tend to look elsewhere, to another place and another time, for a spiritual home. Most of the Byrne immigrants were British, and the century that followed their arrival brought a steady stream of gentleman farmers, second sons and numbers of ordinary, solid Britons to its golden shores. Natal's royalist ruling establishment lobbied against the Union of South Africa in the years before 1910, and popular resistance to the adoption of a contrived South African flag in the 1920s was vocal and occasionally violent. The province is still known as 'The Last Outpost'.

If anything, pro-British sentiment has been even stronger in the provincial capital of Pietermaritzburg, which hugs the green and pleasant uplands about 60 miles inland from Durban. It is a charming little city of Victorian red-brick buildings, wrought-iron railings, roses and azaleas that, as one writer puts it, 'wears its air of grace and quality with becoming ease'. The Union Jack still flies occasionally at its various clubs.

But the colonial past and its human legacy are no longer the arbiters of fashion, character and attitude in Natal. Whites make up just one tenth of the provincial population, Indians a fifth and the black people, predominantly of Zulu (or Nguni) stock, the vast majority. Greater Durban is said to be the world's fastest-growing urban area, its numbers expanding faster than those of Mexico City or Cairo; by far the most numerous of the incomers are poor people from a countryside that can no longer support them.

Tens of thousands of black families crowd the shanty settlements that fringe the western boundaries, and their integration into the urban mainstream is the overwhelming priority and preoccupation of the city fathers. The contradiction of image and reality – of Durban the privileged playground on the one hand, and of a city besieged by poverty on the other – is striking indeed.

A rich diversity of cuisine

Gourmet visitors to South Africa who are expecting to experience a single national cuisine will be disappointed – there's no such thing. The country is simply too diverse in terms of its people and their origins.

Eating habits vary from region to region, and the gastronomical traditions of some of the larger colonial and immigrant groups – Italian, German, Greek, Portuguese and so on – are more firmly embedded in the overall culinary culture than others. Around Durban, for example, where almost a million Indians live, the fragrances of curries, tandoori meats and delectable birianis scent the humid air. Among Cape Town's cosmopolitan offerings is 'old Cape' (Dutch and Afrikaner) fare in which lamb, mutton and venison, sugary vegetables and sticky *konfyts* (preserves) feature prominently.

The Cape is also the home of so-called Malay cooking – a legacy of the early slave community and notable for its scented *bredies*, made from among other things mutton, onions, crushed chilli and tomatoes,

Durban's yacht basin and its leisure craft, with Victoria Embankment in the background. The area's many attractions include the Natal Maritime Museum, the intriguingly intricate Vasco da Gama Clock, and the African Arts Centre. From here, pleasure cruisers take you out into the great bay for wave-level views of city, yacht basin and harbour.

Natal's second city and seat of the provincial government is Pietermaritzburg, set among misty hills north-west of Durban. The place was founded, in 1838, by the eastern Voortrekkers just before their victory over Dingane's Zulu army at Blood River. It was named in honour of Boer leaders Piet Retief and Gert Maritz, and served as the capital of the fledgling Boer republic of Natalia until Britain annexed the region in 1843. Pictured is the impressive city hall, the southern hemisphere's largest all-brick building.

This mall is at the junction of Pietermaritzburg's Church and Timber streets.

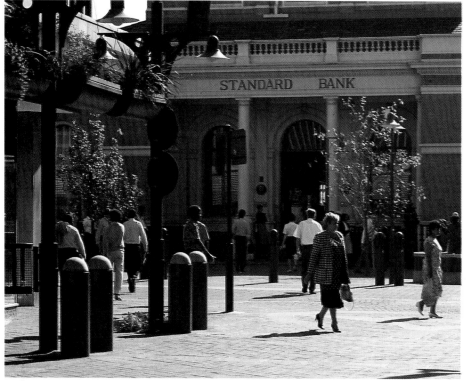

cabbage, pumpkin or piquant *waterblommetjies* ('little water flowers'); for its curry-flavoured *boboties*, its stuffed rotis, spicy meatballs and its lusciously gooey desserts. Cape Malay curries are different from those of Bombay and Madras, being sweeter and more gentle on the palate.

One of the most time-honoured of middle-class South Africa's social traditions is the 'braai' (short for *braaivleis*), a standard barbecue of beef, lamb, chicken and fatty, distinctively spiced *boerewors* ('farmer's sausage'), salads, and potatoes baked in foil. The meat is well marinated, grilled over wood or charcoal and has an appealingly smoky flavour – which changes with the type of the wood used.

Braais are usually held in a sheltered corner of the garden or patio; guests tend to congregate according to gender, with the men gathering around the fire. They are also central to outdoor occasions – beach parties, country picnics, cricket matches and the like.

Traditional African cooking is hard to find outside the remoter country areas, though the occasional gimmicky spread, featuring maybe fried termites and roasted snake, is put on for the adventurous tourist. The standard fare, though, is pretty plain stuff, its main focus being ground maize and boiled meat.

The African peoples have not raised food to cult status, simply because for the vast majority eating is a practical business, and for many of those below the breadline, a formidably challenging one as well.

South Africans are predominantly a nation of beer and wine drinkers. The breweries and the wine industry promote their products with vigour and flair, and they've been helped up until recently by laws restricting many restaurants and other outlets to serving only 'wine and malt'.

All in all, South African wines are excellent and still fairly cheap. Beer is comparatively expensive and there's a great deal less choice – the beverage has been produced under more-or-less monopolistic conditions – but quality is good.

There are few pubs in South Africa that fall into the classic English mould, but most public drinking is done in the lounges or 'men-only' bars of hotels.

Among urban blacks most of the drink goes down in 'shebeens', an Irish word meaning a speakeasy, of which there are well over 5000 in Soweto alone. Once strictly illegal, most of these now-tolerated private drinking-houses are efficiently run by personable 'shebeen queens' who lay on steak, *pap* (maize porridge), *vetkoek* ('fat cakes'), music, dancing, and the

personalised comforts of home. Plus alcohol, of course, at reasonable prices: the lower-class places dispense rugged home-brews; the more stylish ones provide the standard range of malts, spirits, fine wines and liqueur brandies. Several notches above the average shebeen are licensed taverns (Soweto has 200), upmarket clubs and nightspots with names like The Clock Bar, The Cambridge, The A-Train and The Pelican Club, places where – as one writer describes it – 'cool cats dance slowly with elegant ladies, while young bachelors show off their peculiar combinations of streetwalking, African dancing and disco frenzy'.

One fine old Afrikaner country tradition, once threatened with legal execution but which now seems to be making a comeback, is the home-distilling and consumption of rough and potent concoctions generally known as *mampoer* but also called Cape smoke, *witblits* ('white lightning') and *withond* ('white dog'). *Mampoer* can be made from peaches and also from apricots, grapes, pears, potatoes, prickly pears, karree berries or just about any other fruit that lies to hand.

Mampoer has become respectable again – it even has its own tourist 'route', a meander through the Groot Marico/Zeerust district of the Transvaal.

Paradise under threat

Some of the finest of the world's wildernesses are within South Africa's eastern coastal belt – in Natal and Zululand, where the warmth and humidity, and the green luxuriance, provide ideal habitats for great numbers of animals and birds.

A particularly notable reserve is Hluhluwe, which takes its name from the monkey ropes, or liana, that festoon the river banks. It consists of a lovely swathe of misty mountain forest, grassland slope and dense riverine bush which together sustain an amazing diversity of animal and plant life. Adjoining Hluhluwe is the Umfolozi Game Reserve, the reserves

After decades of enforced separation, people of different races are finally beginning to discover each other; game reserves, especially, provide the kind of informal atmosphere conducive to easy social intercourse.

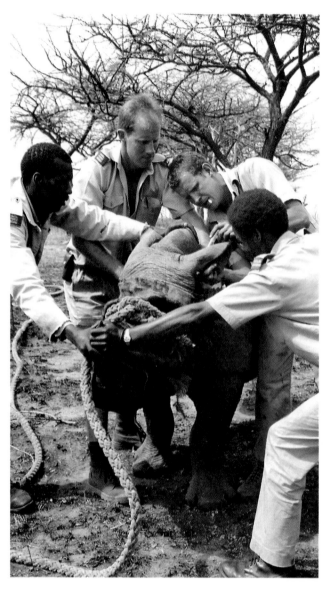

Umfolozi vets take sample blood from the ear of a captive white rhino. The reserve has been in the vanguard of the campaign to conserve this species, together with its smaller, more aggressive and rarer black cousin.

The endearing red duiker (Cephalophus natalensis), *a secretive little browser that is at its most active after night falls. It stands just 17 inches high at the shoulder.*

– all in Natal and Zululand. The extinction of the species seemed imminent, but an ambitious and deservedly well-publicised rescue and breeding programme – inaugurated in the 1960s and led by the renowned conservationist Ian Player (the brother of the world-famous golfer, Gary Player) – turned the tide for the survival of the white rhino. Endangered elsewhere, it breeds especially well in the Umfolozi reserve, to the point where surplus animals can be translocated to other reserves within and beyond South Africa's borders.

Special, too, are the lions of the Umfolozi reserve, who are there almost by accident. Much prized by the late-Victorian 'sporting' hunters, they had become regionally extinct by the turn of the century, but some 60 years later a solitary male, for reasons known only to himself, beat an erratic and elusive 250 mile path from Mozambique to the Umfolozi area. In due course a small group of females was introduced, cubs were born, and the pride flourished.

Quite different in character, but in its way even more impressive than the Hluhluwe-Umfolozi com-

separated by a narrow strip of land, known as The Corridor, across which game passes freely.

The Umfolozi and Hluhluwe reserves are the oldest of South Africa's game parks. They were proclaimed in 1895, three years before the Transvaal's Sabie Game Reserve – forerunner of the Kruger National Park – came into being. Their story, though, almost ended in tragedy. The region sustained great numbers of game but, by the same token, attracted many cattle ranchers. The close proximity of wild animals and domestic stock had an unfortunate outcome: the tsetse fly that thrived among the game brought the dreaded nagana disease to the cattle (akin to sleeping sickness, which the tsetse fly causes in humans) and, in 1929, a ruthless extermination campaign was launched. In all, some 100,000 wild animals were slaughtered during the 20 years to 1950, when the killings were finally abandoned in favour of more effective chemical controls. Owing to the strenuous efforts of dedicated conservationists, the numbers of game rapidly increased.

Among the Umfolozi's more special residents are more than a thousand white rhino, the largest concentration in the world – which also represents something of an environmental triumph. At one time there were just 30 or so of these animals known to be in existence plex is the Greater St Lucia Wetland Park, close to Natal's eastern seaboard. This comprises a number of closely interrelated areas – the lake, the estuary, wetlands, coastal forest, some of the world's highest sand dunes and, of course, the sea.

The 140-square-mile 'lake' (in reality a series of lagoons running into the estuary) is on average just three feet deep and its teeming fish, insects, crustaceans and other nutritious creatures draw vast numbers of birds – over 350 different species in all, among them white pelicans, herons, flamingoes, saddlebill storks, rare Caspian terns and a breeding colony of fish eagles.

Farther afield, but still part of the complex, are the dune forests and marshy grasslands of Cape Vidal, the deep, green, magical Dukuduku Forest, the ecologically fragile Eastern Shores reserve and, running up the coast, the St Lucia and Maputaland marine reserves, together covering an enormous 340-square-mile area. Leatherback and loggerhead turtles nest in the northern parts; the lovely offshore coral reefs are some of the world's southernmost.

All this amounts to an environmental paradise, one of the richest on earth, but, like so much else that is perceived as 'non-productive', it is vulnerable to social and commercial pressures. Homeless people have moved into the Dukuduku Forest – they have an ancestral claim to the area, and they are a community in desperate need of homes but, still, their presence poses a threat to the indigenous forest.

In 1989 a private mining company announced plans to strip-mine the dunes of the eastern shores of Lake St Lucia. There was a public outcry; a million people signed the protest petition and the danger was temporarily averted. The issue, however, remains in the balance until the findings of a comprehensive environmental impact study are made known.

Whether St Lucia and the other components of South Africa's precious natural heritage can survive the short-term industrial and housing demands of the future remains to be seen.

Echoes of the old tribal ways

The destruction of the old social order of Africa began with the European conquests of the last century and is being completed, in the present one, by mass-migration to the cities, where the ways of the black man's forefathers are engulfed by Western cultural norms.

Fragments of the tribal past have managed to survive the onslaught, though. Here and there, mostly in the remoter rural areas, one glimpses the measured formalities, the subtleties and strident colours of another place and time. The girls of Venda still collectively perform a sensuous, sinuous snake dance to mark their entry to womanhood. Xhosa boys whiten their bodies with clay, and don reed costumes and masks in preparation for the adult life. During the

White rhino in the Hluhluwe Game Reserve. Despite their short legs and massive bodies – an adult male weighs up to 6000 pounds – these animals can move at a surprisingly agile 25 mph over short distances.

Young Venda girls perform the python dance, or Damba, as part of their initiation into adulthood. Venda, in the north-eastern Transvaal, is one of the four 'independent' states created within South Africa by apartheid.

Enormously elongated toes characterise the African jacana (Actophilornis africanus) – a feature that enables the bird to stand and walk on floating vegetation. In flight, its long legs extend far beyond the tail.

year's first new-moon phase, the Swazis of KaNg-wane hold their Great Incwala, a complex six-day sequence of ritual, endurance test, song and feast that signifies the rebirth of their chiefs, reaffirms national identity and celebrates the first fruits of the soil.

Some Ndebele women wear metal anklets and necklaces that can never be removed, and paint the walls of their homes in bright geometric patterns that were devised a long, long time ago. Among the rolling hills of Transkei a particular application of red ochre and a style of red blanket define status, and men and married women smoke long, carved tobacco pipes. Travel through the dusty byways of Natal and you will come across beautifully made beehive-shaped huts of

The colourful style of the traditional Ndebele. Some of the ornamentation the women wear – including the rings around neck and lower legs – cannot be removed.

Ndebele homesteads are usually rectangular, thatched and boldly decorated with geometrical patterns. The distinctive designs are finger-painted by the women.

the Zulu craftsmen, many-coloured beaded head-dresses, and men in splendid ceremonial regalia that speaks of a long-gone and perhaps prouder age.

Visible remnants of the ancient cultures are everywhere, but they are becoming fewer by the year, and a great deal of what you do see is specially laid on for the tourist. More enduring are the abstracts – language and folklore, belief and decorum, and the strong bonds of kinship.

The Zulu are the largest, and to outsiders best-known, of the African peoples, a six-million-strong nation that has retained its royalty, guarded its identity and nurtured its traditions, though oddly enough many of these – certainly the military ones – don't go back all that far. Less than 200 years ago the Zulu were one of the smaller and weaker segments of the eastern Nguni, a loose linguistic and cultural association of about 800 different groups and clans. But then a brilliant and determined young man named Shaka succeeded to the chieftainship and set about changing the balance – by ruthlessly reorganising the small Zulu army and its weaponry.

A major element of this transformation was the *Amabutho* system of regiments, graded according to age and each with its own living quarters, its uniform and insignia. Another was the assegai, the short stabbing-spear that forced warriors into close combat. Up until then, 'battles' had often been rather polite affairs, the weaker side gracefully retiring after a token exchange of throwing spears. Above all, Shaka developed fighting techniques to a finely honed science, dividing the *impi* (group of warriors) into a 'chest', for frontal assault; and two 'horns', for encirclement – a lethal arrangement that proved devastatingly successful. Within the next few years the Zulu had defeated and absorbed neighbouring clans and were in control

Xhosa women of the Transkei. The way the headdress is wrapped will indicate age, status and occasion; the white facial smears are applied only for special occasions.

of almost the entire eastern seaboard. Raiding *impi* were ranging beyond the Drakensberg, and the cataclysmically destructive migration of peoples, known as the *Mfecane*, or *Difaqane*, was in full flood.

The power of these incredible people, though, lasted only a short while. Magnificent discipline and raw courage were simply no match for the guns and laagers of the invading Voortrekkers and in December 1838, after a series of fierce engagements, the Zulu were routed at Blood River. They lived in uncomfortable peace with the white man for the next four decades and then, in 1879, fought the last of their major wars. At Isandlwana they prevailed, wiping out an entire British force; a few weeks later, at Cetshwayo's capital of Ulundi, they were defeated.

The traditional Zulu still maintain the system of age sets. Male ceremonial dress is a colourful outfit of shield and stick and sometimes spear, a kilt of 'tails' made from animal skin, fur and the feathers of the widow-bird; on the head more feathers, ostrich plumes and, if the man is married, a head-ring. Earlobes are pierced to 'open up the mind' and, in the case of married men, patterned wooden plugs are inserted.

Both sexes wear a great deal of beadwork on gala occasions – around neck, arms, hips and ankles. The beads, which are a fairly recent, European-introduced addition to costume, are stitched together in intricately ornamental designs, the patterns and colours taking on symbolic significance. Those of the man are a sort of love-letter, telling of the esteem and affection of the woman who made them for him. Colours have precise

meanings (though these vary from area to area), conveying joy and sadness, wealth and poverty, loyalty (royal blue), purity and love (white), marriage (black), red for the weeping of the eyes, and so on.

In tribal life marriage is arranged between the parents and kinsmen of the betrothed; the bride-price (*lobola*) is raised by the groom's family and nowadays paid in hard cash, though occasionally – as it used to be – in cows and oxen.

Cattle, hoe-culture and hunting – but especially cattle – were central to the Zulu economy. Meat, however, was regarded as a delicacy, to be eaten only on special days – the cow was more important for its milk and its hide and, beyond those, for its mystical significance. It served as the sacrifice through which the deities were approached, as the link between the generations and, in the form of *lobola*, as the binding agent between families. Just how cherished it was is apparent in the language: over a hundred different terms were applied to different types of cattle and their distinguishing characteristics; praise poems were sung in their honour; the cattle-kraal was sacred.

In the old days Zulu men were assigned the duties of warrior, hunter and stockman; the women cultivated the fields, harvesting crops of maize, groundnuts, pumpkins, grain sorghum, taro and other tubers. The brewing of beer, the making of pots and baskets, cooking, cleaning and the gathering of firewood were also part of the women's lot.

Ancient religious conviction exists alongside orthodox Christianity among the Zulu and, in common with the religions of other African peoples, has four basic elements. First of all there is the belief in a Supreme Being, *Nkulunkulu*, the great-great-one, who is creator of all things but, like the lesser Lord of Heaven (*Inkosi phezulu*, the bringer of thunder, rain and light-

This young Zulu girl is almost of marriageable age. In the old days the bride-price (or lobola) *was paid, by the groom's family, in cattle; modern betrothals are usually sealed with cash.*

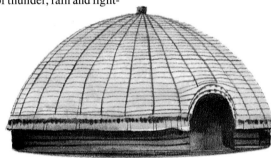

ning) and the Daughter of Heaven (*Nomkhubulwana*, an entity associated with early spring, the growth of corn, and fertility), is considered infinitely remote. Much more approachable are the ancestors, who are believed to exert a profound influence on their living descendants and are therefore to be both venerated and propitiated. There is also a generally animistic outlook, which endows things like rocks, rivers and trees with a spiritual presence, and there is the enduring authority of the spirit medium (the *sangoma*), who acts as intermediary between the living and the dead.

Zulu weddings and other ceremonial events are joyous affairs, spectacular in sight, sound and movement. Musical instruments are few and basic – cowhide or goatskin drum and perhaps reed pipe – but there is the powerful, deep-throated roar of the men's

The traditional Zulu beehive-shaped homestead, with its extensive thatching held together by grass ropes. The huts are usually built around a central cattle kraal, which is considered sacred – the only women who are allowed to enter are the daughters of the family.

The Little Karoo's huge Cango cave complex was once home to the ancient Bushmen – and to countless generations of bats, whose petrified bodies litter the floor of one particular area. The illuminated halls are now a prime tourist attraction.

Below right: Although the boom days are long gone, ostriches are still farmed in the Little Karoo.

voices in part harmony, the high descants of the women, the clapping of hands and stamping of feet and the pulsating motion of massed dancers swaying rhythmically together.

On other occasions there is the shouting of praises, composed in honour of a chief or *induna* or indeed anyone who deserves the accolade of his peers. These laudations, known as *izibongo*, are part of the body of Zulu epic poetry, which in turn belongs to a wider tradition of oral literature that also encompasses folk-lore and love-songs.

The fluctuating fortunes of the ostrich feather

In the days when feathers were all the rage among ladies of fashion, fortunes were made and extravagant lifestyles followed in and around the southern Cape ostrich-farming town of Oudtshoorn.

The boom years lasted from around 1870 to the beginning of the First World War; at one stage London buyers were paying £90 for a pound of white plumes, and the local breeders prospered, building themselves

times more generous than a hen's egg). A visit to one of the farms makes a pleasant outing; among the more intriguing attractions are the 'ostrich derby' track races in which visitors can also take part.

Oudtshoorn is the capital of what is known as the Little Karoo, which is not to be confused with its much bigger and bleaker sister to the north. The region, a low-lying strip of attractive and in some places rugged country, lies between the southern coastal rampart and the grand Swartberg range to the north. It doesn't receive a great deal of rain, and much of the land looks dry, but in fact the soils are rich and moist from the Olifants River and the perennial streams that flow from the uplands. The ostrich flourishes here, but so too does walnut and grape, wheat and lucerne and fields of ripening tobacco.

Prime tourist attraction of the Little Karoo is its labyrinthine Cango Caves complex, 17 miles north of Oudtshoorn. Cango One has 28 chambers festooned with a fantasia of strangely sculpted, often strikingly coloured stalactites, stalagmites and other calcified limestone features, including one column that rises a full 41 feet. The Grand Hall is well over a hundred yards in diameter.

The dripstone formations in Cango Two, named the 'Wonder Cave', are especially beautiful; Cango Three extends a further 1750 yards; Cango Four and Cango Five, lower down in the sequence, are still being charted, and there are other systems in the area that await exploration.

mansions in the most decoratively lavish of styles – ostentatious affairs of turrets, gables, miles of wrought-iron filigree, sweeping staircases, silken drapery, teak panelling, French wallpaper, Italian marble and Persian carpeting.

The bubble burst in August 1914 when the outbreak of the First World War put severe constraints on cargo ships travelling from South Africa to England. Furthermore, after the war demand for South African ostrich feathers slumped: the growing popularity of the motor car was discouraging women from wearing large, feather-laden hats, and the United States had also begun breeding ostriches and exporting feathers in competition with South Africa.

Today a few of the original 'feather palaces' can be seen in the area, though the more elaborate of them are no longer private homes – they've been turned into museums, hostels and old-age homes. Ostriches are still farmed and today there is a steady demand for plumes for use as fashion accessories and in household dusters. This biggest of all birds has other uses: ostrich steak is tasty and becoming increasingly popular, its skin is turned into luxurious leather goods, and its egg is nutritious and large (in omelette terms, 24

These ostrich chicks will grow up to become a valuable source of leather for shoes and handbags, feathers for household dusters, and dried meat, known as biltong.

A stunning aerial view of Cape Town and its distinctively flat-topped mountain massif. On the right is Lion's Head.

Boys competing in the South African Nippers' life-saving championships, held at Fish Hoek on the Cape Peninsula's False Bay coast.

Cycling is a prominent feature of the Cape weekend. This cyclist is taking part in a major triathlon event at Gordon's Bay, just down the coast from Cape Town.

The fairest of Capes

'Away from Cape Town I live in exile,' wrote Lawrence Green, one of South Africa's most prolific and well-known literary figures. 'For me it would be an evil turning of life's wheel if I were forced to end my days elsewhere.'

Many Capetonians – the more privileged ones at least – feel the same way, and indeed they have a great deal to be thankful for: the sheer physical grandeur of the place, the blueness of the sea, the broad sweep of Table Bay and the buzz of the waterfront, magical forests that cover the inland hills, the many amiable eating and drinking places, and a laid-back, unhurried pace of life that their upcountry cousins don't really understand but tend to envy.

And the mountain, always the mountain. Its immensity looms above the city, the summit being almost two miles of straight-edge flanked by Devil's Peak and the sugarloaf of Lion's Head. On clear days this distinctive trinity can be discerned 120 miles out to sea, though all too often the heights are hidden from view by the 'tablecloth', consisting of great white billows of cloud that tumble down the massively precipitous northern face. At these times the mountain takes on a sinister, threatening personality, which is embodied in the local legend of Van Hunks, an old pirate who fought a tobacco-smoking contest with the devil (this produced the clouds) and still lurks today to frighten small children.

The first recorded climb of Table Mountain was in 1503 by the Portuguese explorer Antonio da Saldanha, who had to beat his own way through the wooded krantzes to the top. Today there are over 350 established paths, some of them gentle, others strenuous, and a few downright dangerous – the mountain regularly takes its toll of human life.

Most of the more than half a million people who make the ascent each year take the easy way up – boarding the cable-car, which has been making the six-minute trip for over half a century. From the crest there are magnificent views of Cape Town, its harbour and the bay below, of the Twelve Apostles (a row of craggy peaks that stand sentinel-like along the Peninsula's western seaboard), of False Bay and the blue-grey Hottentots Holland range of mountains and, to the south, of Cape Point. Near the cable-station at the summit are a restaurant and souvenir shop (from where letters bearing the Table Mountain postmark can be sent) and plaques describing the walks, the nature reserve and the plants that grace the slopes. Nearly every one of the Peninsula's 2600 floral species grows on the slopes and the plateau behind.

Cape Town huddles in the amphitheatre formed by the mountain, a small city by world standards but neat, self-composed, cosmopolitan and bustling. Flower

The small-spotted genet (Genetta genetta) is anathema to the country's chicken farmers. This small, nocturnal and adept hunter of rats, mice, lizards, snakes and frogs also has a particular taste for domestic poultry.

Part of the Victoria and Alfred Waterfront development, a massive scheme to bring in the tourists, and to reunite Capetonians with their historic harbour area.

sellers do a raucous trade on Adderley Street, while Greenmarket Square, the Grand Parade and the rather attractive railway station forecourt are busy and bright with fleamarkets.

Adderley Street – it was named after a 19th-century British politician who helped stop an Australian-type convict settlement scheme at the Cape – is the main thoroughfare. At its upper (mountain) end are lovely public gardens that began life as the first Dutch colony's vegetable patch. They now hold over 8000 different kinds of local and (mostly) exotic plant and are fringed by some grand buildings – the Houses of Parliament, the South African Museum, the Great and Old Synagogues, the South African Library and the South African National Gallery.

Long Street, which runs parallel to Adderley, was once the fast-beating heart of Cape Town. It's a bit seedy now, lined with junk-shops, fast-food outlets and the like and, at its upper end, with boarding and bawdy houses, but lively enough and still quite elegant in parts. Many of the buildings are of late Victorian vintage, charmingly filigreed legacies of the wrought-iron age. They and others like them in other parts of the city are being given facelifts with delightful results, though the work usually falls short of full restoration – 'facadism', the gutting and modernisation of everything inside the original shell, is the trend. And a fair number of even earlier houses have survived intact, whitewashed edifices with huge teak doors, green-shuttered windows, terraces with corner seats of stone and the glimpse of a vined courtyard.

Much of the Cape Town of even quite recent memory, though, has vanished altogether – some of it beneath what is known as the Foreshore. This testament to poor town planning replaced the beach, seafront palms and a beautiful old pier with functional office blocks, petrol storage tanks and a raised highway that cut Capetonians off from their beloved harbour. But some of the colour and vitality are coming back: city and sea have been joined together again by the imaginative and ambitious Victoria & Alfred Waterfront project, an exciting enterprise that draws its inspiration from successful harbour rejuvenation schemes in San Francisco, Baltimore, Sydney and elsewhere.

The more interesting of the old buildings have been converted in the pierhead area to serve as hotels, restaurants, bistros, pubs, theatres, an arts and crafts market, and speciality stores. There's also an excellent fully operational little brewery. The new Victoria Wharf houses about 100 shops, 13 eateries, 11 cinemas, a wine centre and fish and produce markets. There are also open quaysides, a yacht basin, marina, public squares, promenades, walkways, waterways, a steam railway station and an aquarium.

The Waterfront isn't just for leisure activities – it continues to function as a working area, a nuts-and-

One of Cape Town's many fleamarkets. It is thought that the so-called 'informal economy', a sector that embraces backyard industry, township taxi services, street trading and other unregulated activities (including some that are illegal) generates around 30 per cent of South Africa's domestic income.

Many members of Cape Town's Islamic community live in the inner suburb of Bo-Kaap (right), a visually enchanting area of small, flat-roofed 18th-century houses. A small museum in the area recalls the days under Dutch control when the Muslims were forbidden to practise their religion – and were forced to hold prayer services in secret.

bolts harbour for commercial fishing vessels (which provide the authenticity). The University of Cape Town's Graduate School of Business has moved into the revamped Breakwater prison; offices and accommodation are all part of the grand design.

Along with Table Mountain, Cape Point far to the south, and the gracious homesteads and vineyards of the Constantia valley, the Waterfront now ranks as one of Cape Town's major drawcards and part of a sustained campaign to put the city firmly onto the traveller's map.

Cape Town's skies are unpredictable, with the city sometimes seeming to pass through all four seasons in a single 24-hour period. The long winters are wet and chilly and summers are hot and dry, with long, cloudless days which are occasionally perfect in their somnolent stillness. However, these days are all too often fractured by a gusty, unnerving 'black' south-easter that sometimes reaches gale force and thoroughly disrupts enjoyment of the outdoors. Yet without the 'Cape Doctor' (the wind is said to cleanse the city of sickness by blowing away pollution, dust and insects), summertime Cape Town would be uncomfortably humid.

The best months are those of the short spring (September and October) and the slightly longer autumn (March through to May), when the wind drops to nothing, the sun is gentle on the skin, colours are changing and the fragile air lifts and sustains the spirit.

A part of the old city that remains historically intact is the Bo-Kaap (literally, 'above the Cape'), a suburb of pretty little flat-roofed 18th century houses set on the slopes of Signal Hill and home to a community of Cape Town's Muslims. The area is commonly but quite incorrectly referred to as the Malay Quarter. Many of the residents are descendants of the slaves and a sprinkling of aristocratic political exiles from Malaya, Java, the Celibes and other Indonesian islands. They are a devout people with their own distinctive customs, cuisine and cultural traditions, among which is the *khalifa* sword-dance – though it has now lost much of its religious significance and is only performed occasionally, as a spectacle.

The folk of the Bo-Kaap belong to a much larger Cape society of both Muslim and, more numerously, Christian faith who were until recently classified as 'coloured'. Traditional home to about 50,000 of these mixed-descent people was Zonnebloem, better known and remembered as District Six, a vibrant, colourful, densely packed inner suburb that in 1966 was declared a 'white area' under the apartheid laws, and then demolished, its residents moved to the brand-new, characterless town of Mitchells Plain and to other areas on the wind-blown Cape Flats. Only one or

Devout Muslims leave their mosque. Those members of the Islamic community who can afford it, make at least one pilgrimage to the Holy City of Mecca.

two buildings – churches and mosques, without their congregations – escaped the bulldozers.

Situated right next to the city, Zonnebloem is prime real-estate, but the property developers have kept their distance for fear of alienating its previous inhabitants and the area has remained a wasteland for more than two decades – a grim and silent reminder of the suffering caused by the country's racial laws. Now it is to be returned to the people, and it may, just possibly, regain something of its old magic.

A floral wonderland

The winter-rainfall countryside of the southern and south-western Cape covers just 0.04 per cent of the earth's land area but the terrain is so incredibly rich in plant life that it is classed as one of the world's six botanical regions, enjoying peer ranking with the great Boreal Kingdom that extends over North America and most of Europe and Asia.

The Cape Floral Kingdom contains about 8500 different species, most of them low-growing, evergreen shrubs that flourish in habitats ranging from mountain tops to coastal sands. All are hardy and adapted to withstand long summer droughts. Of the 8500 species, 6000 are unique to specific areas; over 120 different species have been found growing in a single 100-square-yard patch in one of the nature reserves.

The vegetation type has several names – Cape scrub or 'macchia', sclerophyllous bush and, most commonly, *fynbos*. Some of the floral residents – among them the orchids, disas, lilies, red-hot pokers and especially the heathers (ericas, of which there are over 600) and proteas – are very lovely. The last-men-

The exquisite Disa uniflora, *or 'Pride of Table Mountain', an orchid that graces the moister parts of the south-western Cape's mountains.*

Far right: South Africa has 13 genera and 368 species of protea, most of which are found in the fynbos *(heath-type) countryside of the Cape. Family members range from the lovely little marsh rose to the tall silver tree. This is* Protea aristata.

tioned are named after Proteus, the Greek god who changed his appearance at will, and indeed the plants are amazing in their variety. The king protea is South Africa's national flower.

The tallest member of the protea family is the silver tree whose green leaves have a pale sheen – imparted by silky hairs – that is at its most noticeable and most entrancing when the foliage shimmers in the breeze. According to legend, the tree will only grow within sight of Table Mountain, but in reality is found farther

afield in the south-western Cape and has in fact been successfully cultivated in Europe.

As with so much of South Africa's natural heritage, this floral wealth is coming under increasing pressure, its chief enemy being ever-encroaching man. There is also competition from alien flora, and the proliferation of the aggressive Argentine ant, which has steadily taken over from its indigenous cousins, which played a vital role in the reproductive cycle of many of the plants by disseminating their seeds far and wide.

Spirit of the vine

For a few days each autumn a motley but quite distinguished crowd – merchants, individual buyers, collectors, investors, aficionados, journalists and others with a good (or at least plausible) reason for being there – gathers in the grounds of a lavishly proportioned country home called Nederburg, 37 miles north-east of Cape Town and the venue for the annual invitation-only South African wine auction.

It's the premier event of its kind on the local calendar and, for a fair number of those present, a deadly serious business: all the leading Cape estates put their best on show; some excellent vintages are up for bidding, and a great deal of money changes hands. But

The magnificent, mountain-fringed Hex River Valley is one of the most productive areas of the winelands: heavily irrigated, intensively cultivated, its 200 or so farms yield most of the late-maturing grapes that are exported from the country.

Harvest-time in the vineyards. Altogether, some 5000 Cape grape-growers cultivate more than 3000 million vines; the most prominent cultivars are Stein (also known as Chenin Blanc), Cinsaut, Columbar, Palomino, Muscat d'Alexandrie (Hanepoot) and Clairette Blanche. There are also some low-volume, high-quality varieties, including Cabernet Sauvignon, Riesling and Chardonnay.

it's also a lively social occasion, and many of the guests have come along for the sheer fun of it – for the food and wine stalls, the generous tastings, the fashion parades, for the carnival atmosphere and conviviality in the warm sunshine.

Nederburg is a large, gabled and supremely elegant country mansion built in 1800, in the heart of what is known as the Boland, a region of grand mountain ranges, gentle plains, vineyards and orchards heavy with fruit, of old towns, villages and homesteads.

This was the first of the country areas to be colonised by the Dutch: they began to filter into the traditional Khoisan lands to the east and north of the Cape outpost in the 1660s and were well enough established by the end of the next decade to found a permanent settlement – the now substantial and very attractive town of Stellenbosch. In the years that followed, valley after valley was settled. The farms flourished, and their owners spread themselves: they extended their modest pioneer-type houses, changed the roof-pitch to accommodate a *solder* (gabled loft), built on wings, added stables and coach-houses, a *buite kamer* (outside room) for the eldest son and quarters for the slaves. By the end of the 17th century a distinct style of architecture was beginning to emerge: thick-walled, lime-washed, thatch-roofed houses with a strict and appealing symmetry about them.

Some had imposing front entrances surmounted by gables and flanked by evenly-spaced, green-shuttered windows. Inside was the *voorkamer*, a spacious front room often divided by an elaborately carved wooden screen that could be folded back to make space for larger gatherings. Leading off were the bedrooms and,

at the back, the less formal *agterkamer* (back room) and a barn-like kitchen equipped with large open fireplace, stinkwood (or yellowwood) furniture and galleries of iron and gleaming copperware. The overall style had something of old Holland about it, something of the France of the Huguenot refugees (who had arrived in the later 1680s) and something of the East Indies, but it matured in its own way, over the decades, to become recognised and respected as Cape Dutch.

Some exquisite Cape Dutch homesteads have survived the centuries, most of them dating back to the middle and later 1700s, fewer to the early 1800s. Nederburg is a fine example but by no means the biggest and best. Grander by far is Vergelegen, the indulgence of a spendthrift early Cape governor. Scores of these places are open to the public, mainly by way of the various wine routes – these being leisurely itineraries devised on the lines of the French *Routes de Vin* and the German *Weinstrassen*.

Altogether nine such routes have been established (though four fall outside the Boland) and they provide an excellent means of exploring both the countryside and the world of wine. Most of the cellars offer tastings and tours, a few have museums and craft shops, some run cordon bleu restaurants, others serve plainer fare, such as cheese platters, and everywhere there are farm stalls fragrant with fruit, home-style preserves and the distinctive local cheeses.

As a guest at the homestead you have the opportunity to talk to people who know all the secrets and subtleties of wine-making, take luncheon in the dappled shade of a vine-covered terrace and then go on to the next estate. The pace is undemanding.

This sketch of Cape Town's Groot Schuur ('great barn'), now the State President's official residence, illustrates the 'Cape revival' style set in the 1890s by the celebrated architect Sir Herbert Baker. Some of the features he popularised were crafted teak inside and the traditional gable outside.

The Tulbagh district, first settled in the 1740s, is famed for its vineyards and its lovely Cape Dutch homesteads, among them Uitvlucht, Twee Jonge Gezellen and, pictured here, La Rhone. The town of Tulbagh was badly damaged by an earthquake in 1969, but its buildings have been meticulously restored. Those on Church Street – 32 of them in all – comprise the largest single group of national monuments in South Africa.

South of the Sahara

Dawn has just broken. Through the sun's already dazzling
glare, arriving plane passengers are able to make out a broad curve
of red earth marking the frontier between Saharan Africa and the
lands to its south. The plane comes in to land, and the disembarking
passengers are rapidly swallowed up in a swirl of bright colour,
welcoming smiles and loud laughter. It is clear immediately that
they have arrived in a world of ready spontaneity, yet rooted in
mankind's most ancient past. For, as all the evidence shows, it was
on the African savannas many millions of years ago that humanity
was born, and to this day Africa seems to possess a special spirit,
both young and old at the same time, both wise and carefree.

Nomads coax their herds of zebu and goats through the bush. Because of the droughts which have hit the north in recent years, they have moved further and further south. They have running battles with local farmers who are afraid that the herds will destroy their crops.

Previous page:
From an early age, children are given chores. Those from poor families leave the village to work in the fields. Others go to town and work as errand boys or domestic servants.

Millet and sorghum are the main crops in South-Saharan West Africa. Millet, often used in place of rice at the family table, ripens in the autumn, several weeks after the end of the rainy season. The grain separated from the leaves, is then stored for the winter.

When the baobab loses its leaves, they call it the upside-down tree because, they say, it is the roots and not the branches that point to the sky. Some baobabs are more than 2000 years old and count among the world's oldest living plants.

Towns and Savannas

Visitors to Grand-Bassam, the old seat of government on the Ivory Coast, are still acutely aware of the city's colonial heritage. The European cemetery, sandwiched between the shoreline and the main highway, bears testament to a white population decimated by yellow fever. Despite its time-worn appearance the city retains much of its original charm: it is easy to forget that this was once the centre of the slave trade, or the 'ebony trade' as it was sometimes known euphemistically. The bush that surrounds the old city shimmers in the heat when the sun is at its peak and echoes with sounds which epitomise the country's dark past – the yelp of hyenas, the call of vultures, animals whose existence depends on death and dying.

At least fifteen times the size of the United Kingdom, West Africa stretches from Senegal in the west to the source of the Nile in the east. It comprises 15 countries ranging in size from Mali to tiny Sierra Leone. The frontiers which so fragment this region – borders defined in colonial times and ratified in 1963 – do not reflect any geographical, political or ethnic sense. They are lines drawn on a map by competing European powers in their plunder of Africa.

The countries of West Africa are subject to a variety of climates, which result in starkly contrasting landscapes. The north is dry and arid, with the Sahara desert crossing Senegal, Mali, Burkina Faso and Niger.

There was a time when this region enjoyed regular rainfall from August to September, but in recent years this has dwindled to a few drops which evaporate before they even hit the ground. In one year alone, the desert advanced more than 50 miles, swallowing up acres of marginally fertile land which once supported monkey-bread and tamarind trees, along with other edible plants. Now there is nothing. It is a parched and terrible place where the heat is so intense that the sun glows white. The only people who live here are nomads who travel with their herds from well to well, surviving rather than living – with only vipers, scorpions and hyenas for company.

The coastal strip of West Africa supports a dense rain forest where the air is so waterlogged that survival here is almost as difficult as it is in the north. This area was once carpeted with rare and precious hardwood trees, such as teak and mahogany. In recent years, however, in Gambia, the Ivory Coast, Togo and Ghana, these trees have been hacked down indiscriminately as a cash crop, and where replanting has taken place, it has been with fast-growing softwoods.

To see the true flora and fauna of West Africa today, visitors must travel to one of the national parks – d'Arly or the 'W' Park in Niger and Benin, so-called because the River Niger runs through it in a 'W' shape. Here you can still see elephants, lions and giraffes living in their

In the south of the Ivory Coast, the heavy rains fall from April to July and from November to December. In the towns the streets are flooded, and in the bush, the tracks are impassable.

natural habitat. The national park of Komoé in the north-east of the Ivory Coast and Niokolo-Koba in Senegal are still home to herds of buffalo and antelope; villages in the region play host to hippopotami and crocodiles which the local children are only too delighted to show to visitors. The few coins they receive for their trouble are the sole source of income for the village, apart from the crops.

West Africa relies on agriculture not only to feed itself but also as cash crops to provide needed foreign currency with which other essentials can be purchased. The principal crops are coffee, cocoa, groundnuts, fruit, timber and cotton, and while there is a ready market for all these products, price fluctuations on world markets make economic planning in West Africa a nightmare. In 1989, for instance, pineapples and bananas represented the region's only stable and profitable export. As a result, international aid has become a way of life in West Africa. Cereals are shipped in in vast quantities and local peasants have stopped growing many of the old staples – yams, sorghum, plantains and millet – because there is no longer a market for them either at home or abroad.

Animal husbandry is no more efficient. In times of drought, the nomadic herdsmen regularly slaughter hundreds of animals rather than see them die of thirst. There are a few modern farms but even here the herds are periodically devastated by tsetse flies.

Industrial development in the region has been slow. For years following the colonial period, industry consisted mainly of exporting raw minerals and agricultural products to Europe. More recently, attempts have been made, particularly in Nigeria, to establish steelworks and oil refineries.

The ebony trade

African peoples – hunters, farmers and fishermen – have always lived within their ethnic groups under the control of their kings and traditional rulers. Some of these groups grew and spread to become vast empires, like Ghana which controlled the area between Senegal and Niger until the 11th century; Mali which spread during the 13th and 14th centuries from mid-Niger to the Atlantic; and the Songhay Empire which reigned over the entire loop of the River Niger in the 15th and 16th centuries.

The colonial period in West Africa started in the early 18th century when European powers established rival trading posts along the coast of the Gulf of Guinea. The ancient West African land routes, notably the trans-Saharan, disappeared in favour of the sea. This new structure had many advantages, not least of which was its service to the slave trade.

The colonists did not introduce slavery to Africa. Long before the arrival of European settlers, the Ashanti had used pressed labour in the gold mines which gave the Gold Coast its name. The colonists did, however, develop slavery into a multi-national industry. In the space of 200 years, they were responsible for shipping millions of young men and women to the New World as a labour force for their ever-growing empires.

Near the coast, fish is often the only source of protein. In the country, freshwater fish is caught by men using a round casting net. The women dry and smoke the fish before it is taken to market.

Dwarf hippopotami are unique to the forests of Guinea. They are only one tenth of the size of their big cousins but they frequent the same stretches of water. At night they come ashore and feed off tender young shoots.

The village of Ganvié in Benin
is one of the most picturesque
sights in West Africa.
Sometimes it is possible to
attend the sacred ceremony of
Cokou and see its extraordinary dances beside Lake
Nokoué. From their canoes,
the women of the village sell
fish, avocados, tomatoes,
bananas and nuts. They also
sell fresh drinking water in
huge jugs called 'canaris'.

The huts of the lake-side
villages of Nokoué in Benin
are raised on stilts about ten
feet above the level of the
water. They are constructed of
palm-wood and straw, and are
reached by ladder. Between
the huts, the men place a network of branches to trap fish.

The school house is designed to protect the children from the sun. A current of fresh air passes between the two levels of the roof to keep the pupils cool. The children themselves are responsible for the upkeep of the building.

West African granaries are built in the same manner. They are raised up to protect the contents from rodents. This does not, however, protect them from hungry elephants, who merely flip off the lids with their trunks.

The trade in 'black ebony' suited everyone except those who were actually sold. African chiefs used the trade as a convenient and profitable way to rid themselves of unwanted prisoners; for warring tribes, the capture of slaves became a commercial enterprise in its own right; and for the Europeans – Portuguese, Dutch, French and British – it provided a workforce and untold riches. The trade resulted in the destruction of village life in West Africa. At its height, it was impossible for any young person to work in the fields for fear of being snatched, sold and shipped off to foreign parts.

By the end of the 18th century, there were hundreds of slave-trading posts along the coast of West Africa, and modern Africans are not disposed to forget this terrible period in their history. To begin to understand

ancestry in Brazil as in the United States. Add to these the Afro-American population of Central America, the northern rim of South America and the Caribbean, and it is probable that the population of the New World which owes all or part of its ancestry to Black Africa is probably around 200 million.

That is not all. In many of the countries of the Mediterranean, the Middle East, Iran, Iraq, India and Sri Lanka, and even as far East as China, the presence of Black African blood in the racial mix is quite obvious.

The whole idea of slavery and the forced migration of human beings is repulsive, but the process did make the Black African truly a citizen of the world. And many cultures, both East and West, are the richer for it.

Even when the trade was finally abolished in 1848, European exploitation of the African continent continued. It merely took on a more respectable guise, as merchants, backed by their governments, took countries over lock, stock and barrel.

The rivalry of the European powers created a chaotic situation which was resolved – at least to Europe's satisfaction – in 1884-5 at the Conference of Berlin where, without reference to the native population, a treaty was signed which divided the region systematically. The French, British, Belgians and Portuguese sat round the conference table and allocated vast tracts of land to their respective governments, creating borders and boundaries, most of which survive until this day.

Despite legislation to the contrary, the next hundred years were tantamount to slavery for the Africans. Forced labour in the fields and plantations was little different to that imposed in the cotton fields of Texas and Louisiana. They were compelled to learn the language of their colonial masters, and to become their cannon-fodder in the two great wars.

When the Europeans finally departed West Africa in

The villages which lie in the vicinity of Korhogo, Ivory Coast are noted for their crafts – weaving, sculpture and metalwork. More than 4000 weavers live in these villages and make fine linen fabrics, coloured with a whole range of brilliant vegetable dyes.

The women of West Africa spend hours making themselves look attractive. They wear beautiful cast-gold jewellery. The local goldsmiths take their designs from nature and mythology. Each piece has its own specific significance, sometimes known only to the maker.

the scale and horror of the trade, one should visit the Museum of Slaves on the sinister Isle of Gorée, just off Dakar. The tiny, squalid cells of the fortress seem to be haunted by the souls of the thousands of terrified young Africans who were imprisoned there before being crammed into the stinking holds of ships and transported to the New World.

Centuries of trading in human lives have produced some astonishing statistics. For example, the largest urban concentration of people of African descent today is not in Africa at all; it is in New York City. In the United States as a whole, more than 11 per cent of the population – some 27 million people – are of African descent, a far greater number than in any West African country except Nigeria.

There are at least as many people of African or mixed

the 1950s and 1960s, they left behind a collection of countries with few industries, with little knowledge of modern economic strategies and, more importantly, with very little experience in parliamentary democracy – a system of government which had been imposed upon them. Despite everything, some countries managed to retain a remarkable degree of political stability and economic development. For example, the Ivory Coast became a model for the rest of Africa, thanks in the main to the determination and intelligence of one man, President Houphouët-Boigny, nicknamed *le vieux Boigny*. His success was due not only to considerable personal qualities, but also to the fact that he was the son of a hereditary local chief, and thus a chief in his own right. This birthright commanded more respect among the indigenous population of the Ivory Coast than did any elected or appointed government position.

Great chiefs and small witch-doctors

Many of today's African chiefs are the direct descendants of those chiefs who dealt with the slave-traders and later the colonial governments. Even during the centuries of foreign dominance, local chiefs continued to carry considerable political clout with their own people. Their primary function was to ensure the protection of their community as a whole and to dispense justice to individuals within it. Directly below the chiefs came the representatives of the various trades; and at the bottom of the pecking order came the peasants. Most West African communities had, and still have, a Council of Elders, an elected body which gives advice to anyone who might seek it. It also defines, by established custom, the rights and role of each member of the community, the relationship between castes, and the relationship between men and women.

Family and ethnic ties in rural areas of West Africa are still immensely strong. The good of the majority always takes precedence over the interests of the individual. Personal initiative is discouraged and tribe

Millet is not always ground with a pestle and mortar – these are communal grinding tables in the centre of villages where women meet and gossip while they are working.

The water-collecting huts in the village of Enampore are unique. The drinking water is collected in great earthenware jars where it remains cool.

members are in a constant state of self-examination, wondering whether they are measuring up to the expectations imposed on them by tribal lore.

Many of the countries in West Africa have well established, Western-style democracies, but in all cases, these exist alongside tribal authority and ceremony. There is mutual respect between the two branches of authority, not unlike the relationship between the House of Commons and the Monarchy in Great Britain.

It is this mixture of ancient and modern that makes life in Africa so magical. Modern medicine co-exists with traditional healing, and the witchdoctor or healer is still a powerful figure in many communities. Healers claim to 'communicate with the spirits', using plants, ritual dances, chants and sacrifices, and boast the answer to a host of ailments and problems, ranging from physical pain to impotence. They also carry out quite complex operations without the use of anaesthetics and have been known to achieve results which baffle conventional doctors. Their magic power might be open to scepticism, but apparently their powers of suggestion are not.

In order to become a 'person' – to achieve adulthood – African children must pass a number of tests. They are then ready for their initiation, a ceremony which usually involves circumcision for boys and, in the few areas where it has not been abolished, excision for girls. The rites, which are conducted by tribal elders, are secret and vary in detail from tribe to tribe and caste to caste. The cult of initiation serves a number of functions, both practical and mystical. In the depths of the jungle, or by a roadside in the bush, a youngster will be taught the history and genealogy of his or her tribe, and instructed in the particular role they are expected to fulfil within the community, right down to the trade they must follow. The teaching also acts as an initiation into the secret society of that trade and offers the recipient

protection against evil spirits. Thus, children destined to be blacksmiths – a caste apart in most African societies – learn the secrets of fire and metal, as well as a special language necessary to master his craft.

By Western standards, many of the initiation practices still performed in West Africa are unacceptable. They include the infibulation or excision of young girls to ensure that they maintain their virginity until they are ready to marry. In the Baoulé tribe, the introduction of a young girl to womanhood starts in the evening around the dying embers of the camp fire. In front of the entire village, the girl's grandmother will recount her personal sexual memoirs in graphic detail. She will then demonstrate her sexual

Opposite: Every feast has its own ritual and its own unique mask – the chief's mask of wisdom, the dancer's mask, the clown's mask, the singer's mask, the beggar's mask, and the mask of war.

After the initiation ceremony, children who have not cried, despite the pain, dance their first adult dance to the sound of the circumcision drums. The kaolin with which they are covered not only acts as proof of circumcision, but also helps heal the wounds.

At one time the initiation ceremony took place at the end of the rainy season here in Casamance, Senegal. Now, to avoid interrupting the school year, they take place in the summer.

Senegalese wrestling with all its different blows and holds is a sport which attracts many spectators. Every Sunday in Dakar and its suburbs, you can attend these contests.

Although little known outside their own tribe, chiefs still hold considerable political clout within their community. This is certainly the case with the Emir of Katsina in Nigeria, here parading on his white horse. The life of these princes has changed greatly since the days of the colonial powers. Their function is officially purely ceremonial, but they are seen by their tribesmen as guardians of tradition.

West African drums send coded messages, often holy texts. At certain ceremonies, the drums are only for the ears of the initiates. More often the drum messages are for the gods or deceased ancestors.

granaries, like all those in West Africa, are raised off the ground to protect the contents from rodents. The silos have no doors but are fitted with woven straw lids, like giant sombreros; the elephants flip off these lids with their trunks and devour the contents of rice, sorghum or yams. If a granary happens to be empty, the animals are apt to lose their temper and trample the entire structure underfoot. It is a terrifying and expensive problem for the Somba, and one which keeps their witchdoctors working overtime.

Magic and mythology play a major role in the lives of the Dogon of Mali. Hunted and persecuted for centuries, they live in an almost impenetrable mountain region, the Cliffs of Badiagara. There are three distinct Dogon groups: one lives on the plateau; the second on the rocky outcrops at the base of the cliff; and the third are true cliffdwellers. The Dogon live in villages grouped around a *dogouna*, a shelter housing a council of elders

Northern Nigeria is divided into Emirates, each one ruled by its own Emir. The Emir appears on parade several times a year. At this time, Nigerians can seek pardons or favours from their monarch. It is a wonderful spectacle but the 'Guardian of the Royal Sword' reminds everyone that the Emir is above all else a warlord.

repertoire for the young girl's instruction. This whole performance is supervised by the village elders who sit in the shade of the tamarind trees.

Masks and ritual

Masks play a vital part in West African ritual. They are treasured possessions, handed down from father to son or from mother to daughter. Despite claims to the contrary, the masks sold on tourist stalls are inevitably copies, and usually not very good ones. The masks of Klo which, like many African masks, are imbued with magical properties, are not even allowed on public show; it is thought that their power is so terrible that merely to see them would wreak havoc on the uninitiated.

In the Somba villages of Benin, masks hang outside the people's fortified homes or 'tatas'. Inside the houses other ritual objects abound. Snakeskins, bat wings and pottery shards hang by lengths of straw from the ceiling beams. The masks and other talismans protect the Somba from their main enemy, the elephants which roam the vast 'W' National Park bordering their village and which come marauding after every harvest. Somba

which acts as adviser to the chief. He sits on a low, straw-covered platform, which is supported on poles and is designed to resemble a woman's bosom, the Dogon symbol of fertility.

Dogon village houses nestle among the rocks and feature carved wooden doors and shutters. Each home has its own tiny garden, and together these create a patchwork on the rock face. For a funeral the entire village turns out in full costume, and there is a great deal of dancing and chanting before the body is lowered by ropes to the base of the cliffs and into the burial chambers – the exclusive preserve of the tribal witchdoctors. Dogon men all wear faded, tattered jeans which, for reasons known only to them, protect them from demons.

The beauty and rich culture of the Dogon villages make them popular with tourists. For this reason alone, they are better off than most other remote tribes in the region, and their diet of onions and dried millet is supplemented with luxuries from the town markets.

Most West African villages are still organised along time-honoured lines. Each family has its own small hut; these are placed in a circle around an area of beaten earth which acts as a food store. There is also a kitchen area, a bath area, a children's crèche, a parents' room, and individual sitting rooms for both men and women. Then there are the communal facilities – a hut for guests, a hut for old people, a school and a sacrificial plot – all of which are built and maintained by the community.

Huts and communal buildings are constructed from a mixture of mud and straw and often fall down in the rainy season; since the basic building materials are abundant and free, repairs are neither difficult nor expensive. Living in a 'proper' town house is just a dream to most villagers, whose idea of luxury is a

The beautiful seaside resorts of Senegal cater for tourists from around the world. As far afield as Casamance, you will find villages with guest-houses, basic but comfortable.

corrugated iron roof and a concrete floor. True status is bestowed on anyone who has managed to acquire air conditioning or a car.

Educated Africans realised the need for modernisation. Abidjan, the capital of the Ivory Coast, is a successful example. The city was originally a landlocked village but, in 1950, it was joined to the ocean by the Vridi canal. Today it is a modern city of 750,000 people. Its multi-ethnic population includes approximately 100,000 Lebanese and Syrians and 35,000 Europeans. Abidjan is an important seaport which handles much of the trade from what was French West Africa; for foreigners it provides a glimpse of the West Africa of tomorrow. It boasts the towering Hotel Ivory, several excellent restaurants, an Olympic swimming pool, even a skating rink. But there is another side to Abidjan, as there is to most cities in the Third World. Cross the Charles de Gaulle Bridge (or le pont Boigny) and you arrive in

Treichville, a squalid jumble of shanties and sleazy bars, inhabited by the disenfranchised, mainly young villagers who have travelled to the city in the hope of improving their lot. Few whites, or even affluent blacks, ever set foot in this ghetto, and relationships between the two communities are often strained. It is an old story, and not one which is peculiar to West Africa.

African markets

The real joy of Black Africa is to be found in the village markets with little stalls huddled under matting roofs; the town markets in huge concrete buildings; markets exploding in a blaze of colour and a cacophony of sound. In some towns whole streets are reserved for bakers; others are for butchers, where huge hunks of meat hang from hooks and are eyed hungrily by attendant vultures. There are streets for fishmongers, where the stench is almost unbearable; a street of garden produce, which is a riot of colour with mountains of pawpaws, mangoes, bananas and pineapples; then there are the cereal sellers with their piles of sacks, many

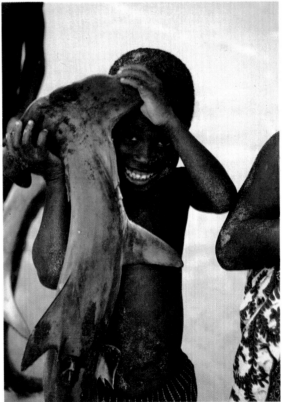

The Atlantic coast and the Bay of Guinea are infested with sharks. To catch them, the fishermen set their nets a few yards from the shore. In Sierra Leone it is believed that shark's teeth have magical properties and they are much sought-after and extremely expensive.

marked with a Red Cross or an European Community logo. The dispensers of potions are there to tempt you with a bizarre array of concoctions – powdered gazelle bones, dried python skins and egrets' beaks – all of which promise long life, health and virility.

West Africa's many peoples meet in the town markets, where a hundred languages and dialects can be heard in as many minutes. The markets are dirty, smelly and hot, but they are an unforgettable experience: an alien world which one enters with joy and leaves with sadness. Everywhere the 'Mammys' sell little toys and trinkets from enormous enamel bowls, or offer little platters of chicken rice. They eat and they chatter; for them this is home.

The markets are the lifeblood of the West African economy, but their effectiveness is damaged by an inadequate infrastructure. Paved roads are almost unknown and the distances covered are vast. Streams of ancient lorries clatter along dirt paths, potholed and repaired with corrugated iron and many other materials. In the rainy season, even these become impassable, and entire regions are cut off for months on end.

A new network of roads is essential if any economic and social changes are to be effected in landlocked countries such as Mali and Niger. The cost is enormous and work is progressing slowly.

The Niger is the largest river system in West Africa with a catchment area of more than 500,000 square miles. The river itself is more than 2500 miles long and is an important line of communication for the entire region, even though it is impassable for nine months of the year because too little water flows in it. In the rainy season it offers the traveller a spectacular journey into the heart of the region. It brushes the sand dunes of the Sahara at the heights of Gao, before wending its way through Timbuktu and back towards its source, where it waters Mopti and the other towns of the Sahel. The Rivers Niger and Bani join in Mopti, and here there is yet another extraordinary market where Peule women, with their stately carriage, and Songhay women, with huge earrings, parade among the stalls. From Mopti, the river winds south to Djenne, the 'Venice of the Sahel' and the site of an extraordinary mosque built entirely of earth and dating from the 14th century.

The River Niger is also an important wild-life sanctuary and is home to hundreds of different types of bird, from the splendid blue heron to the large and ungainly Calaos. Ornithologists from all over the world travel to the Niger for a glimpse of some of the rarest species of bird life. They have to tread carefully because the Niger is also home to hippopotami and crocodiles, neither of which take kindly to being disturbed.

For centuries, the Niger has provided a livelihood for fishermen who work its banks, using strange round nets which they cast over the water with a great sweep of the arm. Sadly, the number of fishermen is dwindling in direct proportion to the fish stocks. Pollution and chronic droughts have wrought havoc on breeding patterns and even the great 'Captain' fish is fast disappearing from the tables of West African restaurants.

Allah rides with the driver

Vehicles take a pounding on the appalling roads and mechanics work around the clock to keep cars, trucks and buses serviceable. Bus stations are always crowded as families scramble for seats on one of the famous 'bush taxis'. Luggage is piled high on the roofs and livestock are tethered to the seats of these ancient

The markets are an accurate barometer of the products of the region. The sea food and shells come from the coastal villages, fruit from the bush, and cereals from elsewhere. Because of the climate and the appalling roads, produce goes straight from the producer to the consumer and is seldom transported any real distance.

vehicles as they lurch along dusty roads to the remote villages of the bush.

Bus stations, like the markets, show West African life in its most optimistic light. Despite the chaos, they are jolly places where waiting passengers stretch out on their mats in the sun and sleep; children shout and play; and mothers breast-feed their babies as they haggle over the price of a bus ticket. The bus driver usually relents and takes what is offered, and then sends up prayers for a safe journey. The ancient buses themselves are daubed with colourful graffitti – 'Allah go with the driver', 'He will go as far as Dakar', 'He has driven right around the world' and 'He managed to get to Paris without a permit'.

If you have time on your hands, the bush taxis are a splendid way of seeing the more remote areas of West Africa; for the Africans, they are the only way home and they suffer their eccentricities with admirable patience. It is not uncommon for the buses to break down, and for the driver to tell everyone to get off and push. Roadside mechanics are abundant. With a handful of tools, a foot-pump and a little knowhow, enterprising Africans have set up shop along the roadside, and they have no shortage of customers for their services. These mechanics – usually teenage boys – are typical of a new

Markets are divided into sections, each with its own speciality. The haggling is intense. The range of goods varies considerably from region to region, reflecting local production. Animals are slaughtered on market day to ensure that meat is fresh.

The influx of tourists to parts of West Africa has brought new trade. Waiters, shoe-blacks, flower-sellers, and car park attendants, are all new professions in modern West Africa.

Japanese motorcycles are a new status symbol in West Africa. In Ouagadougou, capital of Burkina Faso, traffic is hair-raising and motorbike accidents frequently block the roads for hours.

class of small traders. At sunrise, groups of these young entrepreneurs cluster around trestle tables in the street eating breakfast. They chatter about anything from politics, the price of spare parts to local gossip, all the time straining their ears to transistor radios. They genuflect to their elders who make their routine inspection of the area with feudal arrogance. When it is time to go to work, the young men file off to their tiny shops which carry messages in big, crude letters – 'The Peugeot Doctor', 'The Electrician' and 'Here we repair radios and just about everything else'.

The chiefs continue to be the real power in the towns. They dispense justice, and levy taxes with which they maintain a harem, a police force and a small army. In some remote areas human sacrifices are offered at the funeral of a hereditary chieftain. For this reason, there is a general air of panic when any important chief dies. Illegal immigrants and itinerants – people who are not likely to be missed – are all candidates for sacrifice, and they take refuge in the bush until the coast is clear. Some stay in hiding for weeks or even months before they feel that it is safe to return to the town.

The feudal way of life in much of West Africa is spurned by modern, educated Africans. But there is no doubt that it gives a cohesion to community life and acts as a deterrent to delinquency and other forms of anti-social behaviour. Except in the cities, theft is almost unknown; when it is detected, the culprit is summarily executed. Crime is a luxury West Africa cannot afford.

Long live bureaucracy

For the most part, the colonial powers in West Africa let the Africans resolve domestic affairs in their own way. In the last thirty years, as one country after another has achieved independence, some of the new administrations have been less *laissez-faire* about local government. The old chiefs, who have never understood why this new breed of African bureaucrat should have power over them, are sceptical about their suitability to rule. Holding any government post, from lowly customs official to cabinet minister, is seen as an opportunity to line one's own pocket. Those who exercise power have seldom achieved their position through the ballot box, but more commonly through bribery, threats or nepotism. Corruption is rife at every level of officialdom and on a vast scale. At Ouagadougou, in Burkina Faso, after a coup d'état in 1983, the revolutionary council sacked one minister after discovering that he had misappropriated more than a third of the country's exchequer.

Some corruption arises not so much from intrinsic dishonesty, but more from the sheer inefficiency of the system. Customs officials are paid very poorly; they are expected to live on what they can confiscate at the frontiers.

Everyone is affected by this 'underground economy', not least the aid agencies, whose huge contribution is openly misappropriated. Agency officials look with despair as they see their grain sold in street markets at inflated prices, and brand new tractors abandoned by the roadside, stripped bare of parts by young roadside mechanics. They watch as money, earmarked for this or that agricultural project, is squandered by officials on a new Mercedes or a house extension. Corruption is only one of the obstacles to economic and social progress in West Africa. The region is also blighted with drought, administrative disorganisation and incompetence, inadequate transportation, mass illiteracy, and an inflated birthrate.

Nevertheless, the people's *joie de vivre* is infectious. The young follow the latest fashions and adopt the latest political causes. In the evenings, the girls, their hair in plaits of black cotton and decorated with multi-coloured beads, meet their boyfriends at the open-air dance halls where they blend into a riot of living colour and heady perfume. Or they dance in the streets, or go to the pictures, where for two 'sous' they can see the latest

Most trade, including hairdressing, is conducted in the street. Open air kitchens, serving succulent grilled mutton, are particularly popular with tourists.

The mosque at Kano in Nigeria. The Muslim faith rules the life of millions of West Africans. Men visit the mosque five times a day for prayers and the muezzin *acts as a wake-up call in the morning.*

martial arts movie. The younger children have their place in the nightlife, too. 'The Little Bandits' as they are affectionately known, some as young as six, sell hamburgers on the street or act as minders for people's motor vehicles. As night becomes morning, the little bandits go to sleep on the tops of the cars they are guarding, with smiles on their faces. These are the smiles which typify the people of Black Africa. Despite the terrible reality of their lives, and the ever-present threat of drought and famine, they never seem to lose this immense capacity for enjoying life.

Nigeria is both typical and exceptional among the West African nations. It is typical in that it is complex and varied in structure. Its 26 states are home to no less than 250 different and clearly identifiable ethnic groups, each with its own culture and language. The largest of these groups are Hausa and Fulani in the north, who are Muslims; the Ibo (or more properly Igbo) in the east, who are mostly Christian; and the Yoruba in the south-west, who follow a variety of traditional religions.

All these peoples were nominally amalgamated under a common, British authority in 1941. Most of the colonists' investment in Nigeria, however, was confined to the south and a genuine north-south divide was thus created – economically, educationally and technologically.

Since the country gained independence in 1960, the fears and aspirations of the various groups have found expression in a struggle for control of the national government. Even today, more than 30 years on,

conflicts and rivalries between the three major groups – the Hausa and Fulani, the Yorubas, and the Ibos – pose a threat to Nigeria's unity and stability. Against this background of tribal rivalry, however, Nigeria stands alone in West Africa as a modern industrial nation. It has more than its share of problems, but it has the potential to become a truly affluent society.

When the British handed over power in 1960, Nigeria was largely an agricultural nation. It had a certain amount of industry in and around the capital, Lagos, but most of this was government owned and highly inefficient. In the early 1960s, however, the country's economy was revolutionised by the discovery of oil. Initially, the Nigerian government merely exported crude oil, but, by the mid-1970s, it had established several huge refineries.

Within a decade, oil revenues made Nigeria the richest country in West Africa, but the government did not handle its new-found wealth prudently. It used some of the money to build factories and petrochemical plants, but it failed to develop its traditional industries and agriculture. By the time the government realised the need for a balanced and multi-faceted economy, it was too late. There was a glut on the world oil market, and revenues were plummeting. In addition, much of the country's wealth had been eroded by a combination of mismanagement and fraud. By the mid-1980s, Nigeria was facing financial ruin and its economy only survived thanks to massive foreign aid. Today it seems to be back on track, and is slowly building towards a brighter and more stable economic future.

The largest anglicised country in West Africa is Nigeria with a population of nearly 90 million. The discovery of oil and the development of a petrochemical industry makes it the most prosperous country in West Africa. Despite its move into the 20th century, however, Nigeria still adheres to many of the old traditions.

Southern Africa

Dense forests, savannas, deserts, permanently snowcapped mountains and coral seas: such is the diversity of Southern Africa, that swathe of the continent which stretches south of a line drawn from the Cameroons in the west to Kenya in the east. The varieties of landscape are matched by that of the people who live there. It would be hard to find a greater contrast in physical types than between the fine-featured Masai and the squat, stronger-faced Luo and Shona peoples. All share a linguistic tradition known as Bantu – although this cohesion is tenuous since in excess of 600 distinct languages and even more local dialects make up the Bantu family of languages.

The peoples of this region are united by a common history. One theory is that, about 2000 years ago, due to climatic changes or perhaps over-population, a race from the north of Africa moved south via the great lakes. They intermarried with the indigenous population, losing their own ethnic identity but retaining their language which eventually predominated over that of the people they had displaced.

There were several subsequent migrations to Southern Africa. A Caucasian-type people is said to have arrived in the 11th century and is credited with the discovery of copper, tin and gold in today's Zimbabwe, and with the foundation of the Monomotapa empire. A third wave of immigrants, a couple of hundred years later, are thought to have come from Indonesia via Madagascar, bringing with them tropical fruits – bananas, yams and coconuts – which have established themselves as staples of the jungle-dwelling peoples.

Southern Africa was dominated by the Monomotapa empire throughout the Middle Ages, but other black kingdoms flourished during the same period, notably the Congo and Ndongo (now part of Angola). Black supremacy was short-lived. By the 15th century, the European colonisation of Africa had begun. The Portuguese were the first to arrive. In 1460, they established sugar plantations on the islands of Cape Verde and São Tomé. Twenty years later, the navigator Diego Cao discovered the mouth of the River Zaire, and by the end of the century Portuguese monks were well established in the Congo and Angola, attempting unsuccessfully to convert the local population to Christianity. The Portuguese government was less interested in the people's religious convictions than in their capacity for hard physical labour. The indigenous people became, and remained for several hundred years,

Fishermen of the Kisangani area have devised an ingenious method of catching fish in the rapids of the River Zaire. Their hoop-nets are tied to wooden structures with lengths of liana vines. Whether balancing on these rickety scaffolds or steering their canoes through the raging waters, the fishermen show no fear.

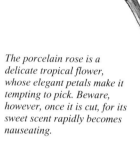

The porcelain rose is a delicate tropical flower, whose elegant petals make it tempting to pick. Beware, however, once it is cut, for its sweet scent rapidly becomes nauseating.

In the villages of Lesotho, the traditional dwellings can be recognised by their circular walls and conical roofs. The Sotho, a farming people, struggle to survive on this infertile and eroded soil.

an ideal slave labour force for Portuguese colonies in South America.

From the 16th century onwards, European colonisation continued unabated. The British, French, Dutch, Portuguese and the Germans all took a slice of the region until, by the 19th century, their control was absolute.

Since the end of the Second World War all the countries of the region have achieved independence. Old colonial names such as Rhodesia, the Belgian Congo and Bechuanaland have long since disappeared from the maps to be replaced by African names such as Zimbabwe, Zaire, Botswana, Zambia and Namibia. But their colonial legacy is still all too apparent. In Zaire, the official language is still French; in Kenya, Tanzania, Malawi, Zambia, Zimbabwe and Botswana, English; in Angola and Mozambique, Portuguese; and in Namibia and South Africa, English and Afrikaans share equal status. Throughout the region, the Bantu languages have been relegated to second place.

The economy and social structures are disparate. Zaire, the biggest country in the region, has a population of 34 million, whereas Botswana is home to just over a million. The mining countries – Zimbabwe, Zaire and Angola – have vast mineral resources as yet under-exploited. Farming is well developed, and the countries of the Atlantic coast draw some income from fishing. Most of the Bantu countries operate subsistence economies. An exception is Kenya which, since independence in 1963, has developed a modern, multi-faceted economy which is the envy of Africa.

The reasons for economic stagnation are manifold.

For the most part, independence was granted grudgingly by the colonial powers, and frequently after years of civil war. The transfer of power was unsettling and new regimes were seldom versed in democratic government, let alone modern economic strategy. Most of the emergent nations borrowed huge sums on the international money markets, which they then squandered, thus saddling their exchequers with debt burdens which continue to grow, as the repayments fall further behind. Then there are bureaucratic inefficiencies, massive corruption, drought and famine, civil wars which span decades, and most recently,

This pride of lions, resting in the shade of a euphorbia, have nothing to fear from their one enemy, big game hunters. They are protected in the Albert National Park in Zaire.

In Zivu, Zaire, sugar cane is one of the main crops. Harvesting takes place in the dry season.

The African elephant is bigger than its Asian counterpart. It can grow to a height of over 12 feet, weigh 7 tons and have a girth of more than 18 feet. In addition to this, its tusks are far bigger, which explains why they have been hunted almost to extinction by ivory poachers.

AIDS, which now affects up to 25 per cent of the adult male population in some areas, decimating their workforces. It is hardly surprising that the region falls short of economic prosperity.

The most ancient people

Southern Africa is home to several yellow-skinned peoples: the Bushmen, or San, the Khoikhoi and, unrelated to these, the Pygmies. The Bushmen and Pygmies are hunter-gatherers, moving from place to place in search of food. Over the centuries, their numbers have fallen from several million to tens of thousands, but they have increasing contact with their black, farmer neighbours, with whom they barter for tools, weapons and agricultural produce.

The Pygmies are perhaps the best known of all African indigenous peoples. The ancient Greek writers Herodotus and Homer both mentioned the existence of these tiny people (adult men average about 4 feet 6 inches). They live between latitudes 5° north and 5° south and are numerous in the dense forest of Ituri in Zaire, where they are known as Bambuti. Other groups live in Ruanda, Burundi, Gabon and the Congo. The Pygmies' skin is a yellowish brown, which although sometimes very dark is still distinct from true black; they have stocky, hairy bodies and short limbs. The men

Little running water does not mean a lack of hygiene. This Pygmy toddler will probably never know the comforts of Western civilisation. Like his ancestors, he will live his life in the equatorial rain forests, feeding himself and his family by hunting and gathering.

Pygmies are monogamous; women enjoy equal rights to the men and both sexes sleep together in huts constructed from branches. Their clothing is basic, and they are one of the few primitive peoples who do not indulge in elaborate self-adornment and jewellery.

Pygmy women are responsible for gathering and hunting moles and snakes, while the men go after bigger game. The Pygmies are masters of their jungle environment and are expert trackers.

Zaire has one of the strongest artistic traditions in Southern Africa. Its statuettes are not objets d'art in the strict sense. Rather, they are magical or religious icons, representing a link between the living and the spirits of the deceased.

Opposite: Bushmen woman drinks from an ostrich egg shell. These huge shells serve as canteens on long journeys or are filled with water and buried as a reserve in case of emergency. Shards of shell are also used by Bushmen to make necklaces.

The main weapon of the Bushmen hunter is the simple bow and arrow. Arrow tips are treated with snake venom, or with poison extracted from plants. The Bushmen hunt in family groups, consisting of the husband, wife (or wives) and their children.

The Bushmen consider all animals to be potential food, with the notable exception of the carrion-eating hyena. Monkey flesh is considered a particular delicacy. When hunters return, the man who has killed or trapped the animal is exempt from work.

are expert archers who hunt in small groups with dogs; the women and children trap smaller creatures, such as moles and lizards, and gather edible plants and berries. Pygmies do not have an original language of their own, but have cobbled one together from the various languages of neighbouring black tribes.

The Bushmen, immortalised by James Uys in his film *The Gods Must be Crazy,* are the original inhabitants of Southern Africa. Today they number only a few thousand and are mainly restricted to the fringes of the Kalahari Desert. Their foraging lifestyle is in decline, and they are now more often to be found working as farm labourers or petrol pump attendants. The origins of the Bushmen are unknown, but it is thought that they are the survivors of the most ancient race still extant: a race which migrated south from the Horn of Africa more than 25,000 years ago. Itinerant and passive by nature, their land was gradually usurped by more determined immigrants, and they sought refuge in the desert. The dramatic decline in their numbers is due in part to disease – brought to the region by Bantu speakers and whites – and partly by their low birthrate. Unlike other African peoples, Bushmen consider large families undesirable.

The Bushmen have their own language with scores of different dialects. It has a rich vocabulary to describe natural phenomena and their religious significance. What makes their language unique is the range of sounds they use – sighs, aspirations and clicks of the tongue – unlike anything in other known languages. After years of research, the Namibian authorities are still unable to produce a dictionary of Ixu, the most widely used of the dialects, in which the syntax does not appear to distinguish between past, present and future.

Like the Pygmies, the Bushmen are short in stature; they have small faces, sloping foreheads, high cheekbones and slanting eyes. True to the prehistoric feminine ideal, a Bushmen woman's beauty is measured by the ampleness of her buttocks and thighs. It is thought that this genetic characteristic developed through the ages as an energy reserve in times of scarcity. The Bushmen age prematurely and their faces are deeply wrinkled before they reach the age of thirty.

The Bushmen religion is animalistic, placing great importance on the power of natural phenomena, and is often celebrated in music. The main instrument is a simple hunter's bow, held in the mouth which serves as a resonance chamber. There are only five notes and no melody, but the music is generally used as an accompaniment for ritual dancers. The Bushmen have countless sacred dances: the dance of the hyena, of the coudou, of the vultures that gather round carcases, and of the zebra. Dancers, adorned with seed anklets, work themselves into a trance-like state; when this is achieved, they are considered to have great healing powers.

The green-eyed baker woman

The Khoikhoi exemplified the 'noble savage' concept so dear to 18th-century artists and philosophers who depicted them in the scantiest of costumes, armed with spears and standing in front of round grass huts. They belong to the great Hamite family and are believed to have originated in Somalia before arriving in Southern Africa some 2000 years ago. They are differentiated from the Bushmen by their traditional ownership of cattle, although they share a similar, clicking speech.

The Khoikhoi no longer exist as a single people, but their descendants include the Nama, who occupy a territory in Southern Namibia between Keetmanshoop and Mariental. Semi-nomadic herdsmen, they work large farms in communities of around ten families and

continue to speak the Khoikhoi dialect.

The baker in the square in Rehoboth (Namibia) has green eyes and is wary of foreigners. Along with some 25,000 other 'Bastars' (bastards), she is of mixed blood. She and her community are the result of the interbreeding between Khoikhoi and Dutch settlers in the 17th and 18th centuries. To avoid persecution and to preserve their identity, the Bastars moved north from the Cape and scratched an existence in South-West Africa (now Namibia). They finally settled and formed a community at Rehoboth in 1868. They are a fierce and independent people, intensely proud of their heritage, which they protect by ensuring that marriage takes place only between members of their own people. They farm and raise Karakul sheep on some 40,000 acres of a vast reservation allocated to them by the Namibian government. Within this reservation, the Bastars have their own Christian church, their own constitution, their own parliament and, within the greater framework of Namibia, their own political party.

Jungles, rivers and deserts

The great forests which dominate equatorial Africa are a direct result of the region's hot, rainy climate. Trees are immense, growing to heights of more than 150 feet, and include such species as kapok, umbrella, limba, gaboon and mahogany. From the sky, the dense jungle looks like an inpenetrable green ocean, yet it is inhabited – the kingdom of the great apes and wild animals such as gorillas, chimpanzees, mandrills, wild pigs and hippopotami.

There are people, too, in the jungles of equatorial Africa, including some of the most prolific and gifted artist-craftsmen of the continent. In the basin of the River Zaire, the native people produce exquisite work in wood, copper and ceramics. They are also gifted musicians who have developed a whole range of instruments over the centuries – horns, whistles, flutes, rattles, bells, stringed instruments and xylophones. Their music has recently been recorded, finding considerable favour in Europe.

Okavango is one of the most extraordinary places in Africa – a water world set in the heart of the Kalahari Desert and swarming with life. Its dominant colour is green: the green of water lilies, papyrus reeds, and of numerous other aquatic plants; the sharper green of the islets; and the bottle green of moss-covered tree trunks and algae-laden water.

This beautiful young Shona woman, from Zimbabwe, will undoubtedly marry according to the rules of her tribe. Her parental uncle will take charge of the negotiations with the suitor's father; her own father will then go and inspect the gifts offered by the fiancé's family. The marriage ceremony will only take place when the business has been brought to a successful conclusion.

Preparing cassava for the table is an arduous task. The roots are rich in starch and are an important staple for many Africans. They are cut into small pieces, dried and then pounded into a fine white flour.

The Kalahari has an area of more than 300,000 square miles, covering the eastern region of Namibia, most of Botswana and south-west Zimbabwe, and encroaching into Angola, Zambia and South Africa. To call it a desert is something of a misnomer. It does have sand, of course: a beautiful red-orange in the south, revealing the presence of iron-oxide; a sinister grey-black in Botswana; and a dazzling white in the Makgadikgadi basin. But the different regions of the

The inhabitants of the semi-desert Cunene district of West Angola depend entirely on the lake for their livelihood. Near the end of its course, the Cunene river forms the frontier with Namibia.

Kalahari are also blessed with a regular, if modest, rainfall of between 6 inches and 24 inches. Vegetation does exist and, even though this is limited both in type and duration, it is sufficient to sustain human life. South-east Botswana, the wettest region of the Kalahari, supports several huge and prosperous cattle ranches.

The Okavango river, the third longest in Southern Africa, has its source in the highlands of Angola, from where it flows south, then east through Namibia and Botswana. In all it travels more than 500 miles and, as it progresses, its form becomes more complex: beginning as a single river, it spreads out into a delta where it teams up with lesser rivers.

The Okavango delta is a region in its own right. Spreading over almost 8000 square miles, it is a mass of islands covered in lush, and often ephemeral, vegetation. These islands are interspersed with waterways which teem with crocodiles and hippopotami. The island of Moremi (75 miles long and 15 miles wide) is the largest single land mass in the delta and serves as a sanctuary for the wild animals who

come from the desert in search of food and water. On Moremi, herds of zebra, lions, elephants, giraffes and antelopes roam unmolested by people, and colonies of ibis, white pelicans and storks skim the water.

Salt pans are desert hollows in which water collects and then evaporates, leaving a thick crust of salt on the ground. Bantu Africa has many of these, the best-known of which are the Etosha in northern Namibia, and the Makgadikgadi in Botswana, 90 miles from the Okavango delta. Since time immemorial, the Bushmen have considered these salt pans as their domain, trading salt for utensils with the neighbouring Tswana. The Bushmen have to endure terrible conditions when they are collecting salt, as the flat, white pans reflect and intensify the stifling heat. When the rains come the pans are transformed. They fill with dazzling blue water, and flamingoes come in their millions to feed on its plankton and mineral salts.

The people who inhabit this savage landscape are not all primitives. Apart from small groups of Bushmen who roam the west of the delta, there are two other, more settled peoples, the Tswana and Herero. Until the beginning of the century, the Herero inhabited lands in the north of Namibia, some 60 miles from the capital at Windhoek. In 1904, however, the German colonial government became alarmed by a rebellion within the tribe and authorised an attack one night. The so-called 'Battle of Waterberg' was not, in fact, so much a battle as an act of genocide. The Germans killed men, women and children in their thousands, and the few hundred

Herero who escaped fled north into British-controlled Bechuanaland (today's Botswana). Some traditions of that period have survived among the Herero people of today, notably the women's bizarre costume. This is an adaptation of the dress adopted by wives of 19th-century German missionaries: the headdress, with its two points, is usually of black or red, while the bodice, with its long leg-of-mutton sleeves, and the ankle-length skirt are multi-coloured in white, green, red, yellow and blue.

Today, the Herero people are the richest pastoral farmers in the region. But there is a branch that lives in the Okavango delta itself. They fish the creeks with lines, nets and harpoons from small two-man dugout canoes called *mokoros*.

The Herero herdsmen, or 'Okavango cowboys', also use *mokoros*, as they drive their cattle aross the river and branches of the delta, prodding them with pole-paddles and urging them on with shouts and whistles. The children help out by making papyrus-reed fires on the river banks in order to steer the cattle away, while the womenfolk, for their part, fish with straw baskets. They work in groups, entirely naked, in the shallows of the delta.

The banks of the Okavango river and those of its tributaries are densely populated but, as one moves away from the water, the desert takes over and the land becomes less sympathetic to human habitation. Here and there are a few small Bantu communities. These desert dwellers live in huts built of reeds and roofed

Crocodiles lay their eggs in the sand of the river banks, then leave them to the mercy of other animals. The weaver bird is more protective towards its young. It constructs complex, pouch-shaped nests which it suspends from the supple branches of trees and bushes.

Fishing with these simple straw baskets requires patience. Sometimes fisherwomen will spend an entire day, up to the waist in water, to catch a single fish. Rather than being eaten straight away, fish are usually smoked over open fires.

with straw, carefully enclosed to protect the people and their livestock from marauding wild animals. Their huts are well spaced and constructed in the shade of occasional trees. None of these villages is big: even Maun in Botswana, the main town of the Okavango, is no more than a handful of reed huts and a few stone buildings.

Mines and waterfalls

In 1902, an English prospector from Bulawayo, William Collier, shot an antelope for his supper. Picking up the carcase, he noticed that the rock where it had fallen was green: a tell-tale green that indicated, to his trained eye, the presence of copper. The deposit proved to be one of Zambia's (then Northern Rhodesia) richest, and the mine still carries the name Roan Antelope, after its discovery. The entire development of Zambia's economy since that time has depended on mineral excavation in this region, which became known as the Copperbelt. In 1991, Zambia was the world's fifth ranked producer. The Copperbelt also yields huge quantities of zinc, cobalt and coal.

Copper was also discovered in Katanga province (now in Zaire) in 1891, but it was not until 1906 that it was first exploited on a commercial scale by a Belgian company, Union Minière du Haut Katanga. A railway was completed four years later, running from Broken Hill (now Kabwe, Zambia) and Elizabethville (now Lubumbashi, Zaire) with the sole purpose of transporting minerals. The province of Katanga became so prosperous that, when Zaire gained independence from Belgium in 1960, it attemped to secede from the new republic under the leadership of Moïse Tshombe. A bloody civil war ensued, which was quelled in 1961 by the United Nations, and Zaire remained a single nation.

Twice as high and two and a half times as wide as Niagara, the Victoria Falls seem to symbolise all that is immoderate on the African continent. In April and May, when the waters are in full flood, they come thundering

Funeral rites vary considerably from one ethnic group to another. But each rite is aimed at ensuring that the deceased's journey to the next world will be trouble-free and comfortable.

Almost everything is carried balanced on the head. These women in the Mossamedes desert in Angola have developed a fine sense of balance and can carry large, ungainly loads in this manner.

down at a rate of almost 100 million gallons a minute, and can be heard more than 12 miles away.

David Livingstone, the Scots missionary and explorer, was the first European to see the falls during his expedition across the African continent in 1855, from Luanda (Angola) in the west to Quelimane (Mozambique) in the east. During his journey, Livingstone travelled along the River Zambezi in a dugout canoe belonging to the Kololo and, on November 16,

he stepped ashore on the island of Kazeruka (since renamed Livingstone) and found himself at the head of the falls. It later transpired that the falls were already known to other travellers and were established in the mythology of Bantu tribes who accorded them magical powers, and regularly appeased them with human sacrifices. The Kololo referred to them as 'Mosi-oa-Toenja', literally 'Smoke that Thunders' and the neighbouring Ndebele called them 'A Manza

The waters of the Zambezi cascade over the Victoria Falls and into the gorges below. David Livingstone was the first European to see the falls in 1855, but they had inspired the local peoples with a mixture of fear and awe long before that. Human sacrifices were made to the unruly powers of the water.

Fungi are another staple for Bantu-speaking Africans. They have developed ways of soaking and cooking varieties which would normally be inedible.

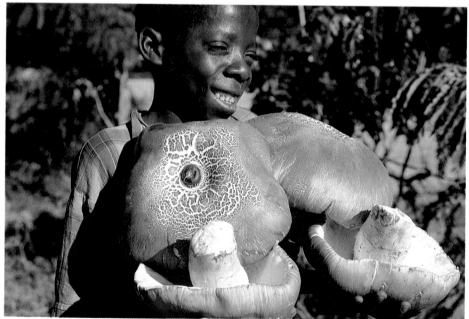

Zambian side, you can see the Main and Rainbow falls, and on the Zimbabwean side you can enjoy the spectacle of the second gorge from the terrace of the Victoria Falls Hotel. This pink-and-white building, a relic of colonial times, was once a favourite watering hole for Rhodesian settlers. The hotel was abandoned during the civil war which finally brought the country's independence in 1980, but has since been refurbished and is once again a fashionable resort for tourists and gamblers. Today's hotel management are happy to lend waterproofs to any guest who feels bold enough to venture through the wild vegetation, past the mighty baobab trees, and into the misty sprays of the great falls.

In the footsteps of King Solomon

Many tales have been told about the fabulous kingdom of Monomotapa, with its fabulous treasure of gold and precious stones. Different stories relate how its history stretches back 3000 years: how it was founded by the Queen of Sheba, or by King Solomon, or the Arabs, or even by the Phoenicians. Perhaps none of these stories is true. What is certain is that at the beginning of the 16th century, Portuguese settlers in Mozambique became intrigued by tales of a wealthy city deep in the hinterland. These rumours were reinforced by the fact that Arab traders were bringing sizeable quantities of gold out of the region which we now know as Zimbabwe. The Portuguese drove the Arabs out of the port of Sofala (Mozambique) and moved inland in search of these legendary riches. They never found them. They had insufficient manpower and resources to establish control of the vast kingdom, which covered the whole of present-day Zimbabwe and a fair part of Mozambique. Even if they had succeeded, they would have been doomed to disappointment. By the time they had arrived, the gold deposits of the region

The equatorial forest is a potential source of untold riches, but felling these massive trees – some of them more than 150 feet tall – is difficult and dangerous. While tree-felling is one of the oldest occupations among jungle-dwelling Africans, there is now considerable pressure from environmental groups for them to earn their living in less damaging ways.

Thungayo', 'The Water That Rises like Smoke'.

Today, even to a jaded 20th-century eye, the falls are an awesome sight. Gushing and foaming, the Zambezi plunges more than 300 feet into the gorges and then pours into a narrow passageway called the 'boiling pot'. Here the river is transformed into a raging torrent. The falls then disappear into a canyon whose presence is revealed only by the rising clouds of water vapour. Over the millennia, the rushing water has hollowed out its bed in the basalt rock, attacking the weakest points, and worked its way into cavities. These gorges zigzag for more than 40 miles before the riverbed joins the plateau, forming a natural border between Zambia and Zimbabwe, and resumes its orderly journey towards the Indian Ocean.

Today's visitors to Victoria Falls can choose from a number of vantage points. From Knife Edge, on the

had long since been mined and the treasure dispersed.

The word 'Monomotapa' seems to have described both the kingdom and its ruler, and 'Zimbabwe' is thought to have referred to the palace or residence of the ruler of that kingdom. Some 17 miles from Masvingo lie the breathtaking ruins of Great Zimbabwe. They are well preserved and serve as ample evidence that a sophisticated community did indeed once exist in the region. The ruins are situated in the middle of a broad valley covered with low savannah bush. On top of a hill is a citadel which overlooks the surrounding countryside. Some 500 yards below are the remains of a large outer wall, dominated by a beautiful conical tower. It is assumed that this wall once protected the royal enclosure. The surviving buildings at Zimbabwe are constructed of dry stones, laid flat or set in a herringbone pattern, creating an intricate mosaic design. Today, trees have grown, dwarfing the ruins and adding

In black Africa, people dance purely for pleasure, but special dances are also performed to celebrate religious festivals and important events in the life of the community.

rather than detracting from an impression of ghostly grandeur.

The true origins of the Zimbabwe ruins still remain a mystery. Archaeological examinations, spanning more than 100 years, have produced a myriad of conflicting theories, but none of them is truly convincing. According to carbon dating, the oldest structures at the site predate the 10th century, but the outer wall was not built until at least 400 years later. The complex stonework was almost certainly constructed by the ancestors of today's Zimbabweans, who were at the centre of a large trading network with the Arabs, who conducted a long and prosperous slave trade within the hinterland of Mozambique's coast. It seems that, during its period of prosperity, between the 14th and 17th centuries, Zimbabwe was the centre of the gold trade, and that the Arabs brought all sorts of objects, shipped in by the vessels of the traditional maritime nations, and exchanged them for gold and slaves: remains of Chinese and Persian porcelain and Venetian glass have been uncovered at the site.

Minerals are by no means Zimbabwe's only resource.

A mask is made in readiness for a ceremony. Shells are often used as eyes, pieces of metal for teeth, and fibres decorated with pearls for the hair.

In Swaziland, warriors in ceremonial dress celebrate the birthday of their king, known as Ngwenyama – the lion. The king is imbued with all sorts of supernatural powers, including the ability to make the land fertile and to bring rain.

It is also a land of plantations. Coffee, tea, cotton and tobacco have all been grown in the Vumba and Burma valleys since the turn of the century, providing the Zimbabwean exchequer with an invaluable additional source of foreign revenue. The valleys are fertile and the climate is mild, even at altitudes of up to 6000 feet. Both the Vumba and Burma were originally settled and planted by a handful of British families and, even since independence, the descendants of some of these families continue to run their estates. And they still live in very much the same manner as they did decades ago, a lifestyle described by the novelist Doris Lessing:

'On Sundays, they meet in chapel, on weekday evenings, at each other's homes. They live in large, white houses, often built with their own hands. Generally the head of the family rises at 5 am. Outside

he joins the plantation workers, who can number up to 100 on the biggest farms and who live close by, grouped together in a cluster of modern buildings forming a 'compound'. The head takes a roll call and delegates tasks to each worker. Then he discusses matters with the black overseer. He speaks English at home and the local dialect with his workers. The biggest event is the tobacco harvest. The leaves are picked by hand and transported in piles to the barns, where they are strung up and left until they are dry. Then the women sort and bundle them.'

Plantations can also be found farther north in the Kivu region of Zaire. Situated at the extreme east of what was once the Belgian Congo, the landscape is dominated by towering volcanoes, the highest standing more than 10,000 feet. The area's beauty and wonderful climate attracted early Belgian colonists who established plantations of coffee, sugar cane and tobacco.

Prior to colonial rule, the vast area that now constitutes Zaire was divided into scores of Bantu-speaking kingdoms. Even today more than 200 identifiable groups have survived. Among the more numerous and powerful are the Bakongo in the west, the Mongo in the central basin: the Baluba in the south and east-central zone; the Luanda in the south-west; the Bashi near Lake Kivu; and the Azande in the north-west.

European explorers first reached this region of Africa in 1484 when the Portuguese, travelling down the west coast of the continent, sailed into the mouth of the River Congo. They did not penetrate beyond the rapids that blocked the river about 100 miles inland from the sea, but they settled in the coastal regions and began to organise a slave trade which was destined to devastate the tribes of the interior for the next three centuries.

It was not until the mid-19th century, and the explorations of Henry Stanley, that the heartland of Zaire was opened up to Europeans. Stanley offered the

In Matadi, a large port and industrial centre in Zaire, the garment workshops employ mostly men. Women are responsible for keeping the house and raising the children.

In Zimbabwe, as in other parts of Africa, a bus trip is considered a great adventure. Departure times are approximate and arrival times beyond conjecture. The buses are crammed full of people and livestock. Luggage is piled high on the roof.

country – not that it was his to offer – to the British, but was rebuffed. Instead he turned to Leopold II, King of the Belgians, who accepted the offer and induced the Berlin Conference (Partition of Africa) of 1885 to entrust him with the personal management of the 'Congo Free State', a territory 80 times larger than Belgium itself. Even by colonial standards, Leopold's rule in the Congo was barbaric and caused such a scandal that, in 1908, responsibility for the territory was transferred to the Belgian government. Over the next half century, Belgium poured massive investments of capital and expertise into the Congo, and in return extracted untold quantities of minerals and agricultural produce.

After the bloody civil war which followed independence in 1960, most Belgian planters and businessmen abandoned the country, and the bigger farms and commercial ventures were either sub-divided or taken over by the government. But more than 30 years later the Belgian influence is everywhere. French is still the official language and is used in administration, post-primary education, and much of the country's commerce.

Big cities, such as Harare (formerly Salisbury), have little to recommend them, particularly if you are poor or unemployed. There is little for the disenfranchised to do except sit around street corners drinking beer out of plastic buckets. Local beer is made from millet or sugar cane and is consumed in enormous quantities.

While the Belgians were colonising Zaire in the 15th and 16th centuries, the Portuguese were settling Angola to the south-west. To them the region was solely a source of slaves, and over the next 300 years, they shipped more than 3 million men and women from its ports to their colonies in Brazil.

There is a strange irony about the Portuguese attitude towards colonisation. While they were the most voracious of the slave-trading nations, the Portuguese viewed their colonies in a different way to the other European powers. Their Assimilation Policy was based on a truly egalitarian principle. Not only were their African territories to be viewed as an integral part of the greater Portugal and their inhabitants to be Portuguese, but they had also a stated aim of creating 'a complete moral, political and economic unity', and interbreeding was actively encouraged. The way to get rid of racial tensions and misunderstandings was, according to official Portuguese, to get rid of races. The ultimate aim was, in theory, the emergence of a mulatto population.

This policy of assimilation remained in effect until Angola and Mozambique gained their respective independence. However worthy the policy might appear on the surface, it must be seen against a background of assumed European superiority. To be 'assimilated' a black African had to be literate in Portuguese, embrace Christianity, renounce tribal loyalties and put aside traditional native customs and beliefs. Until this state of grace was achieved, the individual remained an *indigena*. He lived under a separate code of laws and was subjected to numerous rules and prohibitions as well as forced labour.

Pious in principle, assimilation remained to the end a fraudulent practice. Fewer than one per cent of all Africans in the Portuguese territories ever managed to attain the status of *assimilados*. And when Mozambique and Angola finally achieved their independence, less than 100,000 of the population of 11 million were entitled to full Portuguese citizenship.

Despite the failure of assimilation, the Portuguese influence is everywhere in Mozambique and Angola. Not only is Portuguese still the official language of both countries, but there are also examples of their architecture, such as the 16th-century Carmelite church at Luanda, and the San Fernando Fort at Mossemedes. These and a host of other buildings serve as a constant reminder of the Jesuits' influence in Angola, and Portugal's military expeditions into the heart of both countries. In the 16th and 17th centuries, the city of Mozambique, the country's former capital, was the most prosperous of Portugal's colonial cities. The entrance to the harbour is still dominated by the citadel of São Sebastião and its adjoining chapel, built in 1558, and the church of Nostra Senhora do Buluarte which stands at the foot of the fortress. How many ships must have sailed past its walls since it was built in 1511. Alongside these early buildings are examples of 18th-century baroque and neo-classical architecture – churches, mosques, minarets, residences and palaces. Sadly, all this splendour served as a backdrop to one of the longest and bloodiest civil wars in African history, and Mozambique was reduced to being another tragic footnote to the history of the European colonisation of Africa.

In Gabon, the inhabitants of the forest are deeply superstitious. They have secret societies who practise magic to ward off evil spirits. Some of their ceremonies involve the use of hallucinogens extracted from plants and flowers.

The Land of Lakes

East Africa is the Africa of story books: of lions, crocodiles and giraffes; of soaring mountains and vast lakes. Like Southern Africa, this huge region, which comprises Kenya, Tanzania, Malawi, Uganda, Ruanda and Burundi, owes its loose cohesion to a linguistic tradition and a common colonial history.

The geography of East Africa is largely the result of a spectacular geological accident, the Rift Valley system, which comprises two fissures in the Earth's crust. The Eastern or 'Great' Rift is more than 4500 miles long and in places 2000 yards deep and 40 miles across. It begins far north of the African continent in southern Turkey, runs through Syria, forming the Dead Sea and the Sea of Galilee, and enters Africa at the southern end of the Red Sea. From there it runs southwards and extends all the way to Mozambique where it enters the Indian Ocean south of the Zambezi River. The other fault, the Western Rift, runs roughly parallel, several hundred miles to the west, for most of its 2000-mile length before veering eastwards to join the Great Rift in Malawi.

The depths of the rifts form catch-basins for water from the surrounding highlands, and the result is a chain of narrow lakes which run the length of East Africa, from Lake Albert in northern Uganda to Lake Malawi which tails off into Mozambique. These are the lakes which give the region its description as 'The Africa of Great Lakes'.

The scale of the lakes is breathtaking. At 400 miles, Lake Tanganyika is the longest freshwater lake in the world and the second deepest, reaching depths of 4710 feet in parts. Lake Malawi, which is dominated by the Livingstone Mountains, runs for 375 miles and is more than 2000 feet deep.

Situated on the equator, and spanning the borders of Uganda, Kenya and Tanzania, Lake Victoria is Africa's largest lake with a surface area of 27,000 square miles (approximately the same size as the Republic of Ireland). Its waters serve as the source of the River Nile, which Egyptian legend had always placed in the distant, snow-covered mountains of central Africa. Never more than 135 feet deep, Lake Victoria is more an inland sea than a lake.

With its papyrus beds, islands, creeks, bays and beaches, it has formed a tropical micro-climate. Hippopotami and crocodiles live on its shores, along with Egyptian geese, flamingoes, cormorants and blue herons. Only around Lake Victoria, in the hills and valleys of Kakamega, can one still find the tropical forest of the *Tarzan* movies, with its monkeys, baboons, wild pigs, water buffalo and eagle owls. The rainfall in this forest region is more than 36 inches a year and the

The sun rises over Lake Ngorongoro in Tanzania, a saltwater lake which is home to huge flocks of pink flamingoes and other birds.

Pelicans fish for their supper on Lake Nakuru in Kenya, using the large pocket under the bill as a landing net.

Clove sprays are the dried flowers of the clove plant. The island of Zanzibar satisfies 80 per cent of the world's demand for this spice.

average daytime temperature is about 33°C (91°F).

Lake Victoria is not merely a wildlife sanctuary, thriving commercial centres dot its shores: Kisumu, on the Kenya-Uganda border, for instance, handles all the coffee from Bukoba in Tanzania and most of the cotton from Uganda.

In sharp contrast to Lake Victoria, Lake Malawi, which was discovered in the early 17th century by the Portuguese explorer Boccaro, is surrounded by sandy beaches and palm trees. Its deeply indented shores form a mass of bays and coves which are ideal for all sorts of watersports. In recent years it has become popular with tourists as the 'African Riviera'.

Interspersed with these three great lakes are scores of lesser but still considerable bodies of water, the largest of which are Lakes Kivu, Turkana (formerly Lake Rudolf) and Lake Mobutu. To the Africans, the lakes are not so much a source of visual delight as a means of transport and a livelihood. Most of them are surrounded by fishing villages, from where native fishermen set out in simple canoes to catch the massive Nile perch, a fish which not only forms the basis of their diet but also provides them with a modest income.

Mountains and foothills

The same geological cataclysm which formed the Rift Valley and the great lakes also threw up a whole range of spectacular, volcanic mountains. The highest peaks are Mount Kilimanjaro in northern Tanzania and Mount Kenya, which stand at 19,340 feet and 17,058 feet respectively and are permanently snowcapped. Mount Kenya offers the visitor the intriguing possibility of standing on the equator and dying of frostbite at the

Hippopotami are plentiful in the lakes and swamps of Amboseli Park in southern Kenya. They spend most of their time in the water, but come ashore to search for food.

The elephant herds in the Tsavo Park in Kenya are growing, a potential problem since their food intake is enormous (some 300 lbs a day) and their bulk can devastate crops. After they have slaked their thirst, these elephants will use the waters to wash themselves down.

same time. East Africa also boasts half a dozen other peaks standing well over 12,000 feet, several of which are still actively volcanic.

To see Mount Kilimanjaro is a matter of luck or patience, for it is shrouded in cloud for most of the time. But it is worth the wait. When the cloud lifts, it is a magnificent sight, with its snow-covered twin peaks silhouetted against a blue sky. When the snows on the lower levels melt, they water swampland at the mountain's foot, an area which is overrun by wild animals. The contrast between the stark heights of the mountain and this lush terrain is almost surreal.

Mount Kilimanjaro acts as a spectacular backdrop for the Amboseli National Park, which lies 20 miles to the north of the mountain, across the border in Kenya. The park has a unique ecosystem and variety of game. Five distinct wildlife habitats are contained within its borders: the seasonal lake bed of Lake Amboseli; swamps and marshes with sulphur springs; open plains; acacia woodlands; and lava-rock thornbush country. Amboseli is the best place in the world to study elephants in their natural habitat, since thousands of them have been driven into the park as a refuge from ivory poachers. Despite their experiences at human hands the Amboseli elephants have become accustomed to safari vehicles and can be watched at close quarters as they go about their daily routine of showers, dust baths and grazing. The park is also home to a vast assortment of other wildlife, including lions, cheetahs, Masai giraffe, buffalo, common zebra, Coke's hartebeest, waterbuck, gazelle and impala.

The gentler slopes of the East African mountains are

Whether herdsmen or national park guides, the Masai tribespeople, superbly draped in their brightly coloured robes, have an unmistakably majestic air.

the setting for scores of tea plantations. In Kenya alone these cover more than 150,000 acres from the foothills of Mount Kenya westwards to Kericho. And in Malawi, they form an emerald-green swathe on the mountain-sides to a height of 9000 feet.

Tea was imported from India just after the turn of the century by English colonists, determined to establish in East Africa the crop which had brought them so much commercial success in Darjeeling. The results exceeded their wildest expectations. Altitude, climate and soil provided perfect growing conditions, and the local labour force quickly learned plantation techniques. Today, Kericho in Kenya is the tea capital of Africa, and tea is the only important source of commerce and employment in the area.

Originally, all the plantations were owned by a handful of European families who became enormously rich and powerful, and the daughters of these great plantation families were looked upon for a long time as the most eligible spouses in English-speaking Africa. As the political and economic climate changed, few of these privately owned plantations remained intact. Today, the majority of the East African tea industry is in the hands of Brooke Bond, the English tea giant. The company's Kenyan offices are located next door to the Tea Hotel in Kericho. Its immaculately manicured lawns run to the edge of the emerald plantations which stretch away as far as the eye can see.

The high plateau

Away from the mountain ranges, much of East Africa comprises a high plateau, which lies at an average altitude of some 3600 feet and is split by the Rift Valley. Although it is a virtually continuous land mass, it is infinitely varied. The central highlands are arid, hot

The leaves of the agave plant provide the fibre known commercially as sisal. Sisal is one of the traditional cash crops of both Kenya and Tanzania, but demand has dropped since the development of synthetic fibres.

Zebras mingle and graze with herds of gnu. This is a form of self-protection for the zebra, since lions will generally attack the gnus, which are more numerous and less fleet of foot.

Lions are well camouflaged by the yellow grass in the Ngorongoro crater. It is possible to pass within a few feet without noticing them, which is one of the reasons holidaymakers are forbidden to leave their safari vehicles.

Once the dominant force in central Kenya, the Masai now live as semi-nomadic herdsmen in the scrub of southern Kenya and northern Tanzania.

and inhospitable: an area populated by herdsmen who wander from place to place, past flaming thorn trees and monstrous baobabs, in their never-ending search for the odd shower of rain and the short-lived green flush that follows it. This scrubland conveys a sense of endlessness of which Elspeth Huxley once wrote: 'you could walk straight across to the rim of the world'.

It may be arid and infertile, but this section of the plateau is also rich with wildlife. Elephants, buffalo, zebras, lions, giraffes and a host of other game wander the Tsavo East and Tsavo West National Parks.

In contrast, on the plateau of Northern Kenya, the Kikuyu farmers enjoy a lush landscape on which they grow coffee, tea, bananas and sisal. Heading east from

this region, the plateau changes its face once more; it becomes tropical, with wild, exotic vegetation as the land falls gently away to the Indian Ocean.

The coast itself is world famous for its miles of unspoiled white sand beaches, palm trees, rocky inlets, and mangrove swamps teeming with aquatic life. The beaches themselves are protected from the excesses of the Indian Ocean by an extensive, multi-coloured coral fringe and barrier reef. An ever-present offshore breeze brings relief from the average daytime temperature of 30°C (86°F), making the coast a holiday paradise.

On the high plateau, some 50 miles south-west of Mount Kenya, lies Nairobi, Kenya's capital. It is an important commercial centre and, with a population of more than 2 million, is the largest city between Johannesburg and Cairo. Nairobi, 'The Place of Cold Water' in the Masai language, is a comparatively new city. The area was not inhabited at all until 1899 when George Whitehouse, the chief engineer on the Mombasa-Uganda railway, chose this papyrus bog as his construction headquarters. Almost overnight his decision spawned a boom town, a ramshackle sprawl with all the gun-toting lawlessness of an African Dodge City.

In 1906, the British colonial offices were moved to Nairobi from Mombasa, and the city made its first steps towards respectability. Today Nairobi has become an international centre with a character of its own. It has all

A young Moran, a warrior of the Masai tribe. Like the Zulu, their reputation as fearless fighters has spread far beyond Africa.

Opposite: *The women of the Samburu people, who are related to the Masai, are strikingly beautiful. It is not unusual for them to shave their heads completely and to adorn themselves with masses of colourful bead jewellery.*

the high-rise, glass and concrete of any modern capital city, but this survives alongside much of colonial Nairobi of the Edwardian era. Perhaps the best example of the architecture of this period is the Hotel Norfolk, from which Elspeth Huxley began her journey to Thika.

Cosmopolitan Nairobi has an array of mosques, temples, churches and synagogues. Kenyatta Avenue, the main street, is lined with offices of the world's airlines and confirms Nairobi's position as the hub of the continent's transport and communications network. Nairobi is also a centre of black independence. In a mausoleum behind the railings of the presidential palace lie the remains of Jomo Kenyatta, founder of modern East Africa. Every year, on the anniversary of his death, Kenyans make a pilgrimage to the grave of the man whom they see as their liberator.

Ancient peoples

It is impossible to talk about the recent history of East Africa without looking back to a gorge in northern Tanzania which is a rich source of information about the origins of the African people and of humankind generally. The Olduvai Gorge has thrown up millions of fossils, most belonging to extinct animal species. It was

The Samburu people live to the north of Mount Kenya. Like the Masai, they are tall and slender, and they share a liking for red ochre body paint.

The Samburu (the word means butterfly) cover huge distances with their herds, the men on foot, the women on donkeys, along with tents and the family's possessions.

here that British archaeologist and anthropologist Louis Leakey discovered remains of early people and ape fossils. From banded sediments in the deep fissures of the gorge, Leakey traced human biological and cultural development from about 2 million to 50,000 years ago. His conclusions were controversial but he turned much of the conventional wisdom about human origins on its head. He proved beyond reasonable doubt that *homo erectus* – man who walked upright – had existed in the region more than 2 million years ago, had lived in cooperative communities and used crude implements; and that *homo sapiens* (modern man) had roamed East Africa at least 100,000 years ago, far earlier than had previously been considered possible. Leakey concluded that these people were nomadic hunters and herdsmen, a lifestyle which is carried on to this day by many peoples on the high plateau of East Africa.

Leakey's discoveries were revolutionary in terms of anthropology, but they give us little insight into the complex structure of the population of modern East Africa. Walk down Kenyatta Avenue in Nairobi and, in the space of a few minutes, you will hear people from almost every language stock in Africa, together with numerous Indian, Arabic and European languages. Yet all these people might well have been born and brought up in East Africa.

It is believed that the most ancient peoples of modern East Africa immigrated into the region. The earliest recorded of these were from Ethiopia about 4000 years ago, when a tall, nomadic people who spoke the Cushitic language moved south with their herds from

The city of Mombasa is built on an island. When Vasco de Gama landed there in 1498, it was already a flourishing Arab trading centre, and, in the old town, the Arab influence is still to be found with narrow alleyways, balconies and heavily carved doors.

El Molo fishermen – their name means poor devils – are to be found on the south coast of Lake Turkana (once Lake Rudolf). They are a tiny tribe who cling fiercely to their way of life.

Lake Turkana (formerly Lake Rudolf) until they reached what is now central Tanzania.

The next wave, the Yaaku, settled in central Kenya about a thousand years later and dominated the region for several centuries. They were displaced by later immigrants, and today their decendants survive in small numbers as the Mokogodo people occupying the forest of the same name north-west of Mount Kenya.

About 200 BC, the ancestors of the present Kalenjin people arrived in East Africa from the Nile Valley. They pushed the Cushites and the Yaaku out of their northern territories and gained control of most of the rich highland area in Western Kenya. This group are the forefathers of several ethnic groups– the Kipsigis, Nandi, Marakwet and Tugen – all of whom still thrive in the western highlands around Kitale, Kericho and Eldoret.

Today the Kalenjin, with a population of around two million, are the fourth largest group in Kenya. They have, for the most part, abandoned their semi-nomadic lifestyle and become farmers. Much of Kenya's tea is produced in Kalenjin country.

At about the same time as the Kalenjin people arrived from the north, hordes of small, black Bantu-speaking peoples were streaming into East Africa from the south

and west. Their descendants include the Kikuyu (3.5 million), the Kamba (2 million), the Meru (1 million), the Luyha (2.5 million) and the Gusii (1 million), together with many smaller ethnic groups. Scattered throughout East Africa, the Bantu make up by far the largest linguistic group in the region.

A separate branch of the Bantu people settled near the coast and were called the Mijikenda. This group is thought to have originated from the coastal region of Somalia, and is said to have once had a great kingdom with a capital of stone buildings, where people lived and farmed in peace. Their dominance ended with the arrival of Oromo (Galla) marauders from the north. These warriors swept down the coast of the Indian Ocean from Somalia until they settled inland of Mombasa, where they are known today as the Orma people.

The Mijikenda survived the Oromo invasions, and today their descendants occupy a swathe of land from the Tana River in southern Somalia down as far as central Tanzania.

Perhaps the best known of all the East African peoples are the Masai. Like the Kalenjin, their ancestors migrated south from the Nile Valley. They arrived in the Lake Turkana district where they encountered the

El Molo fishing craft are fragile, built from palm fibres which do not rot in the alkaline waters of Lake Turkana. The fishermen use the same fibres for their lines.

Fish are hung to dry at Monkey Bay on Lake Malawi. Most of the fish caught in the great lakes is salted and dried, and is eaten throughout East Africa.

Kikuyu women display their wares at the market in Karatina in Kenya. The three traditional forms of dress are the kitenge, a type of sarong, the kanga, a short skirt, and the kikoi, a long skirt. All are made of cotton, dyed in brilliant colours with the batik method.

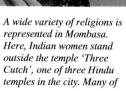

A wide variety of religions is represented in Mombasa. Here, Indian women stand outside the temple 'Three Cutch', one of three Hindu temples in the city. Many of the Indians in East Africa are descended from labourers shipped over from Bombay by the British at the end of the last century to work on the Mombasa-Uganda railway.

Cushites, and it is thought that it is from this meeting that the Masai developed many of their ceremonies and traditions, including complex initiation rites and injunctions against eating most wild game, fowl and fish.

Like the Cushites, the Masai moved steadily south, and by the 14th century they occupied much of the Rift Valley and the adjacent highlands. They became immensely powerful and feared as they raided neighbouring groups, rustling cattle and kidnapping their women. This was still going on when the British first colonised Kenya, and it was not until the late 19th century that the Masai's power was broken and they were driven off the rich farming land to return to their roots as semi-nomadic herdsmen.

Today this proud and dignified people live in the far south of Kenya and number about 250,000. They are the most impressive of the native East African peoples. They are more than six feet, slender and graceful with

their plaited hair, elegant jewellery and distinctive costume. Although they have lost their authority in the region, they have sustained their sophisticated society and have never adopted Christianity or Islam. Nor is their warrior heritage easily forgotten. They still carry spears as they wander the Masai Mara, watching over their herds, and it is said that they still live on milk and fresh animal blood.

The Samburu, cattle herders who live in the Marsabit district of north-east Kenya, are closely related to the Masai and share the Maa language with them, along with many of their customs. They are a strikingly beautiful people who dress in sari-like robes, dyed in vivid colours, wear elaborate jewellery, and are famous as amateur footballers.

Three other East African ethnic groups must be mentioned. The Turkana were warrior-herdsmen who took control of the Lake Rudolf area – the lake has since been renamed after them – and today can be found

Opposite: *The spectacular costume of this Watutsi dancer in Uganda is made from leopard skin and ostrich feathers. His dances reflect different aspects of the hunt.*

wandering around the east of the lake and through the Samburu lands. The Watutsi (or Tutsi) who live in Uganda, Ruanda and Burundi are perhaps best known for their male dancers, many of them over 7 feet tall. They make an awesome sight with their spears and feathered head-dresses, an image of Africa which was adopted by Hollywood. Finally, there are the 2 million Luo people, who make up the third largest group in Kenya. Originally from the Sudan, the Luo migrated into Western Kenya through Uganda in the early 16th century. They displaced or absorbed the indigenous population and then spread south to their present Nyanza homelands. The Luo are a powerful force and after independence they joined forces with the Kikuyu in an abortive attempt to control the government of Kenya.

A taste of Arabia

The Muslim influence in East Africa dates back to the Middle Ages, when Arab merchants from Oman and Persia sailed their dhows down the coast, trading metalwork, glass, ceramics, cereals and wine for ivory, spices, gold and slaves. They made use of the prevailing winds which blew out of the north-east and down the coast for six months of the year and then, conveniently, turned 180° and blew them home again for the other six. The first Arab traders settled on the islands off the east coast of Kenya and Tanzania, mixing with the native black population and giving birth to the brilliant Swahili civilisation. They also settled the coastal mainland but seldom strayed more than 100 miles inland.

The tiny island of Lamu lies in the Indian Ocean, a short distance off the north-east coast of Kenya. Nowhere in the region is the Muslim influence more evident. Today the island's principal town, Lamu, has a population of less than 15,000, yet it boasts a Koranic school and 28 mosques. The calls of the *muezzin* rebound from one to the next from sunrise onwards. The island's status within the Islamic world is confirmed by the two annual pilgrimages to Lamu, which attract thousands of the faithful from other islands in the Lamu archipelago, from mainland Kenya and beyond.

When you climb the steep ladder to the top of the minaret of the Mosque of Sheba, it is easy to see what

The people of Burundi, a small, poor country in the heart of Africa, scratch a living from hunting or from agriculture.

The Watutsi or Tutsi are nomadic herdsmen, like the Masai. They are the most powerful group in Ruanda and Burundi.

attracted the Arabs to settle these islands. Beyond the stone-built town of Lamu lies a panorama of banana and coconut plantations stretching away to a violet sea and beyond that, to the golden sands of the neighbouring island of Manda.

Manda holds the earliest evidence of an Arab presence in East Africa, with glazed pottery from Persia and vases from China confirming that Arab traders were in business here as early as the 10th century. Zanzibar is perhaps the best known and most influential of the Muslim-dominated East African islands. Colonised by Arab traders in the 11th century, it has been an important trading community in the Indian Ocean since the Middle Ages. The great dynasties of Oman established themselves on the island in the 18th century and, when Sultan Seyyid Said assumed power in 1805, he transferred his capital to Zanzibar from Oman and Muscat. This little island is home to more than 300,000 people and the racial mixture – African, white, Indian and Arab – reflects the diversity of East Africa's overall population.

Zanzibar became a British protectorate in 1890 and gained independence in 1963. The Sultan remained head of state until 1964, when he was overthrown by a revolutionary council a year after the island had gained independence. Zanzibar then formed an alliance with Tanganyika and created the new Republic of Tanzania. Despite this, Zanzibar retains a considerable degree of autonomy and preserves its traditions jealously. Its main source of income is the clove. Zanzibar satisfies more than 80 per cent of world demand for this spice.

The Arab influence was not restricted to the islands.

All along the coast of mainland East Africa, one can find mosques dating back to 12th and 13th centuries. But the best example of early Arab architecture is to be found at 13th-century Gedi, nine miles from Malindi on Kenya's Indian Ocean coast. A ghost town, now overgrown by the advancing jungle and inhabited only by monkeys and snakes, Gedi is shrouded in mystery.

A typical thatched farm house in Malawi. Unlike elsewhere in East Africa, there is no antagonism between farmers and nomadic herdsmen in Malawi.

Market day in East Africa is full of colour and noise – a place not only for trading, but also to meet and gossip.

Situated four miles from the ocean, it served no obvious commercial or strategic purpose to a seafaring race. Yet it was once extensive, surrounded by a ten-foot stone wall. In the centre stood a palace, with reception rooms, an audience chamber and more than 40 bedrooms. All roads led away from the palace at right-angles and on these stood luxurious residences – most with a hallway,

private courtyard, four or five bedrooms and a bathroom. Gedi flourished for almost 400 years before it was suddenly and inexplicably abandoned in the 17th century. It is an enigma reminiscent of the ancient city of Zimbabwe. Arab supremacy on the East African coast lasted 500 years, but towards the end of the 15th century the Portuguese started making their first

inroads. In 1493, they set up a garrison at Port Jesus, overlooking Mombasa Harbour. At first this was little more than a stockade but was soon expanded into a full-blown fortress. Thus armed and defended, the new colonists took control of Mombasa and the surrounding region.

The Arabs fought furiously by land and sea to regain control, but their enemies were better equipped and trained and, within ten years, the Portuguese were in control of a long swathe of the East African coast: a supremacy which they sustained with legendary brutality for just over 100 years. Their position was vulnerable, however. Most local tribes sided with the Arabs with whom they had been trading and intermarrying for centuries, and whose religion they had adopted. They cut the Portuguese colony off from the outside world, making it difficult for them to supply and equip their headquarters at Mombasa.

In 1696, the Arabs and their allies attacked Port Jesus. They blockaded the main Portuguese supply route from Goa but, even so, the defenders held out for some 33 months. The eventual loss of Port Jesus spelt the end of Portuguese domination in coastal East Africa. In 1720, they abandoned their colonies and the Arabs re-established their dominance, which they maintained until the arrival of British colonists towards the end of the 19th century.

Today, Mombasa is Kenya's second largest city and its only deep-water harbour. Once a sparsely populated island in a mangrove-lined bay, with Arab dhows bobbing in its harbour, Mombasa is now a thriving container port with all the industrial sprawl that that involves. But the Old Town has been spared this development and still serves as the traditional business quarter and tourist attraction.

Populated by Swahilis, Arabs, Indians and Europeans, Mombasa is still essentially Arabic in

Forests cover more than 20 per cent of the country and communities are small and widespread. Communications are difficult and each village largely runs its own affairs.

character, with its maze of narrow streets and passageways, overhanging balconies and intricately carved doors.

Swahilis and Indians

The word Swahili is of Arabic origin and means 'belonging to the coasts'. It was used by early traders to describe the inhabitants of the islands and coast of East Africa. Today the word more commonly refers to the Swahili language, which is a Bantu language with a lot of Arabic vocabulary. In recent times, a smattering of English phrases (for example, a roundabout is a *kip-lefti*) have crept into the language. Today, Swahili in its many versions is spoken by some 60 million people

The forest of Bugondo in Uganda is not virgin forest, as in the jungles of West Africa, but it does boast huge hardwood trees. The woodcutters work in searing heat and fight a constant war against insects.

Harvest time in the tea plantations of Malawi. The bush was introduced to East Africa from India by the British at the turn of the century. The experiment was a success and tea is now a vital cash crop in Kenya and Malawi.

throughout East Africa, from Somalia in the north to Mozambique in the south, and inland as far as Zaire. It is now accepted as the national language in both Kenya and Tanzania – the media in both countries use both English and Swahili – and it is taught not only in East African schools and universities but also in centres of learning throughout the world. The development of the language has varied in different regions. In the coastal areas and islands it is more influenced by Arabic vocabulary than it is inland. The standard Swahili is based on the Kiunguja dialect (the dialect of Zanzibar, which has also spread throughout Tanzania), but it includes elements from two other important dialects: those of Mombasa and the Kenyan coastal region, and of Lamu.

So who are the Swahili? They are a mixture of Arab and African coastal peoples. Nowadays, many Swahili are Muslims and have Arabic names – Abubakar Khalifa Mamen, for example, or Athman Said. Swahili men tend to be dark-skinned, tall, slender and dignified with finely-chiselled features. In the Kenyan countryside and on the islands of Lamu and Zanzibar, they still wear the traditional ankle-length skirt made from a single length of cloth, long sleeved shirt, sandals and braided skullcap. Youngsters tend to dispense with the cap and wear their hair in explosive 'Afros'.

Swahili women stick even more rigidly to Muslim tradition, covering themselves from head to foot in their 'Buibui', a loose, ankle-length robe which they hold up to cover their faces. This garment is always worn in public as a sign of modesty but is removed in private. It is also discarded when attending 'ladies-only' functions. It is not uncommon for women to take over a cinema or theatre for the evening, when the only men admitted will be the musicians in the orchestra. The auditorium appears as a sea of white-veiled heads until, suddenly, the audience looks up to reveal smiling faces decorated with liberal amounts of lipstick and eye make-up; for Swahili women manage somehow to combine the reserve and dignity of their Arab heritage with the innate gaiety of their black forebears.

Most of the Indians of East Africa originate from Bombay, and many are descended from the 30,000 labourers shipped in by the British colonists at the end of the last century to build the Kenya-Uganda railway. When the railway was finished, the Indians stayed in East Africa and prospered. Today, the Indian community numbers about 85,000 and is concentrated in the big cities and in communities along the Mombasa to Uganda railway. Like the Arabs, they have made their mark on East Africa with their mosques, temples, bazaars and pastel-coloured villas. They have also contributed a great deal to the economic development of the region: many of the businesses throughout East Africa are Indian-owned, and the professions, such as law and medicine, are dominated by Indians.

Today, the majority of the Asian population of East Africa live in Kenya. At one time more than 40,000 Asians lived in Uganda, but they were expelled in 1972 by the dictator Idi Amin. Some fled to Kenya, others travelled to India and England. Since Amin's fall, however, some have returned to Uganda.

Tree leaves are the only form of vegetation suitable for giraffes. Their long necks make eating at ground level difficult, and when they drink, they have to splay their legs wide apart.

Wild animals are protected throughout East Africa. Tourists flock to the game reserves, bringing with them vast sums of badly needed foreign currency.

Islands of the Indian Ocean

Volcanic eruptions produced the emerald paradises of Mauritius
and Réunion; the scattered isles of the Seychelles are the tops of
submerged granite peaks . . . but all have in common the glittering
azure embrace of the Indian Ocean and the many-coloured
abundance of nature at its most exotic, not to mention the interplay
of many different cultural influences. Europeans, Africans,
Indians, Malays and Chinese have all left their mark, as have the
various religions: Christianity, Islam and Hindu. For centuries,
Mauritius was home to the flightless dodo. It lost the race for
survival, but countless other unique animal and plant species
remain for the delight of wildlife-lovers and tourists.

The central plateau of Mauritius is bordered by many impressive mountain peaks. One of them, Rempart Mountain in the south-west of the island, looks rather like a mini Matterhorn. In the foreground is the Rempart River which flows into nearby Tamarind Bay.

French architectural influence is pronounced throughout Mauritius. This house in the small town of Chamarel in the south of the island is a particularly attractive example.

Previous page: *Hindu temples are found all over Mauritius, one of the most ornate examples being the Marianem Temple in Terre Rouge, just outside the capital of Port Louis. The precarious peak in the background, juxtaposed against the spire of one of the temple's domes, is that of Pieter Both Mountain (2690 feet), the second highest on the island.*

Island of Exotica

Less than 400 years ago, Mauritius was a garden paradise, uninhabited by man, in which the dodo roamed – unable to fly because a total absence of predators had finally made its wings obsolete. The dodo is now extinct, its name immortalised in the expression 'as dead as a dodo' and its ungainly form endlessly replicated each year in tens of thousands of tourist mementos. And yet despite the wanton destruction of the dodo and many other species of fauna and flora by the early colonists, Mauritius still retains an enchantment that is uniquely its own.

Mark Twain, when he visited the island at the end of the 19th century, wrote: 'You gather the idea that Mauritius was made first, and then heaven was copied after Mauritius.' It is a notion that Mauritians have taken to their hearts, and his enthusiastic endorsement of the country's charms now appears on the label of one of the island's major exports, Green Island Rum.

Appropriately for the producer and exporter of a fiery spirit, the island of Mauritius has its origins in fire – the island, its dependency Rodrigues, and the nearby French island of Réunion all arising out of a great volcanic upheaval millions of years ago to form what is known today as the Mascarene Archipelago. Weird, precipitous peaks of larval rock, and millions of lava boulders all over the island attest to Mauritius' cataclysmic origins. In time, a coral reef developed along almost the entire length of the island's 100 mile coastline, providing it with placid, fish-filled lagoons and snow white beaches. Shaped like a pear, the island is 40 miles long, and 28 miles wide at its widest point. At the centre of the island is a large plateau punctuated by jagged, volcanic spires.

Mauritius remained uninhabited for millenia – its first recorded sighting being by Arab seafarers more than 1000 years ago who named it Dina Arobi. The island was officially 'discovered' in 1511 by the Portuguese explorer Domingo Fernando and from then on the Portuguese vessels plying their way to India and back started using it as a staging post, releasing monkeys, goats and cattle on the island in order to provide them with more meat on the hoof. The Dutch spent the years between 1638 and 1710 vacillating between establishing settlements on the island and then abandoning them. When they finally lost interest in the island, the French claimed it in 1715 and began colonising it from 1721 onwards. The British took it over by force in 1810, and finally, in 1968, Mauritius became an independent member of the Commonwealth.

Mauritius is exotic in the strictest sense of the word – a great deal of its plants, birds and animals having been introduced from elsewhere. After destroying the legendary dodo, the flightless aphanapteryx, and the magnificent ebony forests, the Dutch introduced such exotica as sugar cane, tobacco, and sambhur deer from Java. They were also reputed to be responsible for the first rats escaping onto the island – with disastrous

One of the most impressive sights in the mountainous Black River district is the Chamarel Waterfall which plunges 330 feet down a cavernous cliff face. This area is also particularly rich in birdlife.

results for the local bird life. Then came the French, followed by the English – both of them introducing a host of new types of animals, birds and plants – such as banyan trees, tea, mongooses, house sparrows and the blacknaped hare from India, casuarina trees from Malaysia (called the filao, locally), aloes and canaries from Africa, and a type of hedgehog, the tenrec, from Madagascar.

Despite the fact that much of the indigenous vegetation of the island has been cleared for growing sugar cane, over 10,000 plant species remain, with more than 150 of these being endemic to the island. Only nine of the original 25 birds found on the island remain today, these include the pink pigeon, the Mauritius fody and the olive white eye. Most of the common birds on the island were introduced from overseas, some of the most frequently seen being Persian nightingales, wax bills, rock doves, mynahs and ring-necked parakeets.

The Mauritian tourist office touts the island as being 'the most cosmopolitan island in the sun' and in this they cannot be far wrong. Mauritius is home to about 1.1 million people, with the Indian population making up just over two thirds of this figure. About a quarter of the population is made up of Creoles, these being the many-hued descendents of the original African slaves, and the offspring of dalliances and marriages between the races.

The rest of the island's inhabitants consists of whites and Chinese, both of whom play important roles in the Mauritian economy. Descendants of the earlier French settlers, the whites hold most of the private wealth on the island and many have powerful positions within the business community. Most of the Chinese community

came from Hong Kong and mainland China during the 19th century. They make their living mostly as retailers or traders – with the majority of the grocery stores outside Port Louis being run by Chinese families.

Religious harmony

On the road leading past the Mahatma Gandhi Institute, situated outside the central town of Moka, is a bronze statue of Gandhi, below which is inscribed the words: 'I am a Hindu, a Muslim, a Christian and a Jew – so are all of you.' If ever a nation has taken these words to its heart, it is surely Mauritius.

There can be few countries in the world where so many diverse religions have existed in such tolerant harmony. At the last count there were more than 87 religious denominations represented on the island – the predominant ones being Hindu (52 per cent), Christian (30 per cent) and Islam (16 per cent). In the capital, Port Louis, the minaret, the spire and the Oriental temple dome all share the town's skyline.

Perhaps there is something in the rhythms of a tropical island that soften the harsher, more intolerant edges of the world's major religions. Islamic fundamentalism finds few enthusiasts here, and caste stratifications are a very pale shadow of what they are in India. Christianity, the religion of most of the Creoles, seems to be rooted less in theological dogma and ritual than in the soil and sands of the island – something tightly woven into the warp and weft of daily existence, rather than being reserved merely for Sunday observance.

It's impossible to drive more than a few miles along a Mauritian road without encountering a shrine to the Virgin Mary, inside which a candle can often be seen burning. Driving around the island, one encounters these sacred spots in the most obscure and unexpected places – deep within a mountain grotto, on rocks at the water's edge, next to streams and waterfalls. Seeing them adorned with flowers, and sometimes with small offerings of food, one has the intimation of a feminine deity who is, for Mauritian Catholics, somehow linked to the cycle of the seasons, and the daily ebb and flow of the tides.

Everywhere, at all times, burning candles. Not only at the shrines of the Virgin, but glowing all night outside Hindu homes inside small glass shrines to the monkey god Hanuman, protector of the home. Driving through small Mauritian hamlets at night, one is struck by the soft glow of scores of these little shrines, topped by the traditional white and red flags of good fortune.

A nation's achievements can be viewed from many points of view – artistic, scientific, economic, to name a few. The notable achievement of the Mauritians seems to be that no matter who the candle burns for, the essential spiritual flame is the same. When Hindu bus driver Rajeh Giandeo starts his descent down through the precipitous Black River Mountain pass in the south of the island, he will as a natural survival reflex (and despite the trident of Shiva dangling from his mirror) offer a quick prayer to the various shrines of the Virgin Mary at the sharpest corners of the pass.

A warm smile of welcome from a pretty boutique owner. Small roadside shops catering for locals and tourists alike are to be found all over the island.

Catholicism is embraced by almost a third of the population and hundreds of shrines to the Virgin Mary are dotted all over the island – such as this one near the sea in the district of Flacq.

A group of young Indo-Mauritians in the marketplace at Curepipe. Tens of thousands of Indian sugar-cane workers arrived in Mauritius in the 19th century. Today, Indians make up the majority of the island's population.

The sweet taste of prosperity

Being stationed on an obscure little island in the middle of the Indian ocean was, for a Dutch soldier in the 17th century, not a terribly attractive proposition. So, in order to help combat the grumblings of the Mauritian garrison, the Dutch East India Company decided that the answer was a plentiful supply of arrack – a fiery spirit which can be distilled from sugar cane.

It was with this particular purpose in mind that sugar cane was first introduced as a crop during the early years of Dutch settlement on the island. With the arrival of the French on the island in 1721, the fields of inferior, arrack-producing cane left by the Dutch gave way to large plantations of top quality cane, which gradually began producing sizeable quantities of sugar

for local consumption and the needs of the ships that regularly called in at Port Louis.

Today, sugar cane dominates the landscape from one end of the island to the other. It is the green backbone of the Mauritian economy, with almost 80 per cent of the island's arable land devoted to its cultivation, and about a quarter of the work force employed in its cultivation and processing. Apart from a sizeable area of state forest reserve in the south, it's almost impossible to drive more than a mile on the island without being surrounded by fields of cane swaying in the trade winds. At the height of the growing season, the ubiquitous cane grows to within a foot or two of the main roads, arching over them, often creating a feeling of travelling through an endless green tunnel.

During the last century there were 250 sugar estates

cane could be planted, the entire rock-strewn surface had to be cleared by hand, and stacked into the rocky piles and pyramids that have become the hallmark of the Mauritian sugar-cane field.

Up until the abolition of slavery by the British in 1835, the work on the cane fields was performed by African slaves. However, once unshackled from their owners, the majority chose to move to the coast where they eked out a modest, but more relaxed living as fishermen. As a result of this sudden depletion of labour, hundreds of thousands of indentured Indians, as well as thousands of Chinese, were brought to the island during the next 75 years. This huge immigration of workers and their families served to alter radically the racial mix of the island, to the extent that the Indian population is now in the majority.

There is a saying in Mauritius – 'May the cane remain forever sweet.' The cane has never lost its literal sweetness, but the intermittent arrival of a cyclone capable of destroying the entire crop, and the unpredictability of the price of sugar on the world market, have been the two Achilles heels that the islanders have had to contend with through the years.

A cane-cutter needs plenty of protection against the heat of the sun and the abrasiveness of the sugar cane. The crop has to be cut entirely by hand – an exhausting task undertaken by both male and female workers.

dotted over the island. However, with the need for greater consolidation, the number has been reduced to 19. Scores of crumbling chimney stacks, often incongruously bristling with weeds and bushes, can still be seen in the plantations – reminders of the days when each estate did its own processing.

Despite the mechanical advances made in the picking of cotton, maize and wheat around the world, no such technological revolution has been made in the harvesting of cane. Each stem has to be individually scythed by hand, making it intensive, arduous work. But the toil involved in cutting the cane today pales in comparison with the back-breaking work involved in originally clearing the fields of rocky debris. Being volcanic in origin, virtually the whole island was covered with black larval rocks, big and small. Before

Consequently, there were various attempts in the past to make the Mauritian economy less dependent on sugar. One of the most spectacularly successful programmes was the introduction of the Export Processing Zone in 1970 which offered attractive financial incentives to overseas manufacturers who set up factories on the island. More than 300 manufacturing enterprises have been set up since then, creating 50,000 new jobs. Within the space of two decades, Mauritius has become one of the world's largest exporters of knitwear, as well as becoming a major producer of many other types of textiles. In fact the eighties must rank as one of the most impressive decades in the island's economic history, with unemployment dropping down to virtually nil by the early nineties.

After sugar and textiles, the third most important industry is tourism – half the number of visitors come from France and the nearby island of Réunion, followed by South Africa, Germany and the United Kingdom. There are around 60 hotels on the island and these collectively service about 200,000 tourists each year.

Buccaneers of the high seas

Sugar has not always been the mainstay of the Mauritian economy. At one time its financial foundation stone was piracy, or privateering. The difference between a pirate and a privateer (also called a corsair) is that a pirate was a freebooter, preying on whatever ships were unfortunate enough to cross his bow, while a privateer was licensed by his country to prey on the shipping of a nation with whom it was at war.

During much of the 18th century, French privateers would sail forth from Mauritius and wreak havoc on British shipping in the Indian Ocean – Britain and France being more or less permanently at war from 1739 onwards. This swashbuckling period represented an economic high point in the island's history. Infamous buccaneers like 'Mad Dog' Deschiens de Kerulvay and the legendary French privateer Robert Surcouf used to sail their ships regularly from the island and return weeks or months later with their holds groaning under loads of booty taken by force from British merchant ships. Mauritian businessmen and sugar plantation owners formed syndicates to finance more privateering vessels, and Port Louis became a thriving *entrepôt,* offering plundered goods at cut-rate prices.

The British tried everything to try to bring the pirates to heel – such as a price of 250,000 francs on the head of Robert Surcouf, dead or alive. But the privateers prospered, and Surcouf himself eventually died in bed at a ripe old age. An Englishman was once heard to criticise Surcouf, saying: 'The French only fight for profit, whilst the English fight for honour and glory.' To which the urbane privateer replied: 'That only proves that each of us fights to acquire something he does not possess.'

The privateers were such a thorn in the side of the English that their unwelcome presence became one of Britain's main motivations for taking possession of Mauritius, which they finally did in 1810 – but only after suffering a disastrous naval defeat by the French at Vieux Grand Port off the south east of the island.

Romance and passion – Mauritian style

There is something about a tropical island that tends to inspire the romantic imagination – and Mauritius is no exception. The renowned 19th-century French poet, Charles Baudelaire, came to Mauritius to get over an unhappy love affair and found the beauty of the local Creole women a great balm and poetic inspiration; another French writer, Bernadin de St Pierre, was so taken by the island's exotic history that he penned the 18th-century romantic classic, *Paul et Virginie.* This tragic couple is to Mauritius what Romeo and Juliet are to the Italian town of Verona. In the climax of de St Pierre's romance, the ship on which Virginie is returning to Mauritius is wrecked off the coast. Her modesty prevents her from taking off her clothes to swim to shore, and she drowns, weighed down by her garments. The tragedy is witnessed from the shore by her adoring Paul, who subsequently dies of a broken heart. A whimsical statue to the couple stands outside the town hall at Curepipe.

Modesty is not, however, the hallmark of the island's most energetic romantic activity – the sega (pronounced 'saygar'). Originating in the days of slavery, this vibrant, courtship dance is one of the unique contributions of the Creole people to the culture of the island. It's a highly ritualised affair: the men wearing tight breeches, the women sporting billowing, multicoloured cotton skirts tucked tightly in at the waist – the better to accent the curvaceousness of their hips. Music is provided by a goatskin tambourine, a guitar fashioned from a gourd, a maraca and a metal triangle.

Traditionally performed on the beach, at night, around an open fire, with the rum bottle doing frequent rounds, the sega starts slowly – initially similar in its rhythms to the samba. As the tempo quickens, enthusiastic onlookers clap their hands, chant, stamp their feet, and throw in ribald comments for good measure. Finally, at the cry of *en bas,* the woman sinks to her knees, arching herself backwards in the manner of a limbo dancer, while the man bends his body over hers, almost touching, but never actually doing so.

A woman sometimes dances for hours at a time, each man taking his turn to captivate her with the vibrancy of his performance. At the end of the ceremony she heads for the man whose lithe, serpentine rhythms have impressed her the most . . .

Port Louis

The capital of Mauritius is Port Louis, situated on the north-western coast of the island, below a number of imposing mountain peaks. It's a vibrant little town of some 140,000 inhabitants in which old, often dilapidated buildings rub shoulders with newer ones. The streets are a noisy bustle of activity during the day; however, in the late afternoon most of those working here return to the less humid residential areas in the higher hinterland, and the central part of the town becomes eerily quiet.

The most attractive part of Port Louis – which was

A pensive, bearded shop-owner at Port Louis' central market – one of the most vibrant parts of the island's capital city. If you're a tourist, taking the time to bargain will often bring down the price of a selected item.

originally called Turtle Bay on account of the large numbers of turtles and tortoises found there – is the impressive, palm-lined Place d'Armes. This avenue leads up from the waterfront to Government House, from the front of which an imposing statue of Queen Victoria gazes sternly out towards the distant horizon.

Somewhat less attractive is the battered, grey stone fort – the Citadel – which looms up monolithically and somewhat menacingly behind the town. It was built in 1835 by the British, who were concerned that their French subjects would rebel against them after they had abolished slavery on the island. The Citadel is, however, a good point from which to take in the entire sweep of the town – including the large race-course that dominates it one side, and to which Mauritians, from all walks of life, flock in their thousands during the racing season from May to October.

The real soul of Port Louis is to be found in its vibrant, colourful, central market which caters for both tourists and Mauritians alike. T-shirts proclaiming 'I love Mauritius' dangle above multicoloured piles of spice-powder, and garishly painted icons of Hindu deities jostle up against attractive spreads of gleaming sea shells, which are imported from the Philippines. The market has burned down on a number of occasions in the past, but it always seems to rise up again, phoenix-like out of the ashes, more vibrant than before. Part of the market is outdoors, another section of it under cover – the latter having the closed-in, labyrinthine atmosphere of a Middle Eastern souk.

For the tourist, the prices with which items are marked invariably turn out to have a certain elasticity – the degree being dependent on how long he or she has to devote to the transaction. For the poorer members of Mauritian society, the time to shop in the market is at the end of the day – when damaged or overripe fruits and vegetables are on sale at greatly reduced prices.

Mauritian essence

Mauritius is a fusion of east and west, an interwoven tapestry of the sights, smells and sounds of Europe, Africa, India and the Far East. The late Pierre Renaud, one of the island's most celebrated writers and poets, captured its quintessential essence when he wrote:

It lies open to the winds of all civilisations
A gigantic leaf floating on the sea . . .
A rainbow made up of the collective breath of its
humanity . . .
Land of cocoa, vanilla and cloves,
Land for all seasons,
A land for all men.

The Company Gardens, with its benches and shady banyan trees, is a cool and welcome refuge for workers in Port Louis. The statue in the foreground is that of Remy Ollier, a 19th-century journalist who was a champion of the coloured people.

Emeralds in the Ocean

Uninhabited by man until the second half of the 18th century, the Seychelles islands lie scattered, like randomly tossed emeralds, across a wide area of the western Indian Ocean just below the Equator. The building of an international airport two decades ago finally opened up these tropical islands to the world – yet despite the stream of foreign tourists that now visit them each year, the Seychelles has thankfully lost little of its spectacular beauty and romantic allure.

There can be very few places left in the world that still qualify for the term 'unspoilt paradise' – but the Seychelles is certainly one of them. Endless white beaches basking in the somnambulant shade of coconut palms, casuarinas and takamaka trees, mist-shrouded granite cliffs rising vertically out of lush tropical forests, and a pond-like, aquamarine sea brimming with a visual feast of exotic underwater life – all combine to create one of the closest things to heaven that one is ever likely to find on earth.

In the Seychelles there are no dangerous animals, poisonous spiders or venomous snakes; no prevalence of tropical disease, and no uncomfortable extremes of heat or cold. There is no real poverty to speak of (it's almost physically impossible to go hungry amidst such a natural abundance of fruit and marine life), and the tourist industry has so far had little impact on the natural beauty of these islands. This is due in part to strict policies laid down by the Government, one of the sanest being that no hotel is permitted to exceed the height of a palm tree.

Situated between 4° and 10° south of the equator, the Seychelles consists of 115 islands, the core of this widely scattered archipelago being located 1000 miles from the east coast of Africa – hence the islands' tourist slogan 'Unique by a Thousand Miles'. And the Seychelles certainly is unique – being the only granite-based islands in the world.

Geologically, the Seychelles are merely the peaks of a vast submerged plateau that once joined Africa with India. In a sense, these islands represent the highest tips of a small continent that didn't quite make it above the surface of the sea. Flying between the main islands, the lower reaches of this submerged land mass can be clearly seen about 150 feet below the sparkling surface. The vegetation of the Seychelles offers an insight into its geological origins – some of the trees and plants echo those of Africa, while others reflect those found in the Orient. Many species of flora found in the islands are, however, dramatically different from anything found in the rest of the world – such as the *bwa mediz,* a plant that is so botanically unique that a completely new family of plants had to be invented in order to classify it.

Most of the Seychelles islands still remain uninhabited by man, and even the half dozen most populated ones are so unspoilt, so lush with natural vegetation, so primal and untouched by their

Idyllic, palm-lined beaches of powdery white sand are the hallmark of the Seychelles. The abundance of reefs around the islands make the beaches amongst the safest in the world – there are no threatening currents or dangerous sharks.

inhabitants, as to scarcely seem possible. Driving along the narrow, winding, well-maintained tar roads that encircle and criss-cross the main island of Mahé is to drive for the most part through what seems like one vast, natural, tropical park. Apart from some modest tea plantations in the higher reaches of the island, and the ubiquitous copra-bearing coconut palms, there is little evidence of any serious agriculture, and hardly any sign of industry – except along a small strip of coast between the capital city of Victoria and the airport a few miles to the south.

The main industry of the Seychelles is in fact tourism – which accounts for 90 per cent of foreign exchange earnings and employs about 20 per cent of the country's active work force. Yet despite the Seychelles' heavy economic reliance on holidaymakers, a strict policy of moderation is being applied to future tourist

A bountiful, silver harvest from the sea. Fish caught in the calmer waters within the lagoons are usually modest in size, but in the open sea beyond the reefs, larger game fish can be found in abundance.

Fishing is something with which virtually every boy or man in the Seychelles is familiar. Apart from the popular fishing methods of netting, trapping or hooking, there is always spearing – a method favoured by youngsters.

development. A five-year plan initiated in 1989 allowed for an increase of only 500 hotel beds on all three of the main islands (there were 3500 beds available in 1989) – with the added proviso that any new hotels built should be limited to 100 beds. At present the number of tourists visiting the islands is fewer than 100,000 a year – a fraction compared with the annual influx into popular Mediterranean islands such as Majorca and Mykonos.

The colourful Creoles

The population of the Seychelles is overwhelmingly Creole, their multi-hued origins lying in the fraternisation that occurred between the French settlers and their African slaves since they first arrived in 1770 on these hitherto uninhabited islands. The British took over the islands from the French in 1814, and later in the 19th century, the population of the islands was considerably increased by the arrival of thousands of Africans freed from slave ships by the British Navy. Evidence of other races who found their way to the Seychelles – from as far afield as India and China – can also be seen in the features of many of its people.

There are probably few societies in the world as racially integrated as that of the Seychelles. Although in the past, there was some sort of class division based on race – the *grand blancs* (white colonists) at the top of the pile and the *noirs* (black labourers) at the bottom – this social stratification has more or less disappeared.

Although French and English are understood to some degree by most of the Seychellois, the *lingua franca* of these islands is Creole – a pleasing, sing-song French patois that originated in the early colonial years as a

With hardly any motorised vehicles on La Digue island, the ox cart remains one of the most popular forms of transport. In the background is one of the charming corrugated iron homes which are a feature of the main Seychelles islands.

Opposite: *Natural minerals and simple designs combine to give many homes in the Seychelles a timeless charm – such as this house in a grove of coconut palms. The climate is so mild that simple wooden shutters are often favoured above glass windows.*

means of communication between slave and master, and between the slaves themselves.

Words used in Creole have been borrowed liberally from English, from the original tribal languages of the African slaves, and also from Arabic. However the language is predominantly French in flavour with the grammar simplified, pronunciation of certain consonants hardened, silent syllables dropped completely, and the soft 'j' used in French becoming a 'z'. Thus 'good morning' is pronounced 'bonzour' instead of the French 'bonjour'; 'this is beautiful' would be 'sa i zoli' instead of 'c'est joli'.

Coups and countercoups

The Royal Swazi Fokker F28 which landed at the Seychelles International Airport at 2.30pm on November 25, 1981 initially aroused little interest. To all intents and purposes, the passengers – a large group of sturdily-built men wearing T-shirts bearing the words 'Ancient Order of Frothblowers' – looked like a rugby team on a group vacation. But when a bored customs official desultorily peered into one of their suitcases and spotted the butt of an AK-47, all hell broke loose.

The 'Ancient Order of Frothblowers' turned out to be a 45-man mercenary force, trained at a secret location within South Africa, whose purpose was to overthrow

Copra is one of the principal agricultural exports of the Seychelles. Here it is being collected in the traditional way – slicing open the coconut with a firm blow from a machete, and then scraping out the white flesh with a metal scourer.

the one-party government of France-Albert René. After a brief shootout at the airport, the mercenaries hijacked an Air India Boeing 707 that had unwittingly landed in the middle of the fracas en route to Bombay, and ordered the pilot to fly them back to South Africa.

The failed coup served as a vivid reminder that below its relaxed, easy-going surface, the Seychelles has often been a tropical hotbed of intrigue and plotting, with attempted coups sometimes coming thick and fast. Two of the main protagonists since the country obtained its independence from Britain in 1976 have been a pair of former law firm partners, James Mancham and France-Albert René. Mancham was the first prime minister of the country after independence; René took over the country in an almost bloodless coup a year later while Mancham was attending a conference of Commonwealth leaders in London. Mancham in turn was thought by many to have been behind the South African mercenary force that attempted the abortive coup in 1981. There was a mutiny of NCOs in the Seychelles army in 1982, and various bombings and political murders the following year. In 1984 another coup attempt was foiled, and in 1986 there was an attempted coup by a cabal of majors within the Seychelles army.

The fact that the islands are of considerable strategic value gives an added dimension of unpredictability to the political equation. The US has a permanent presence on the islands in the form of a 'non-military' satellite tracking base; Soviet missiles are believed to have been installed as part of the islands' defence system. And both US and Russian warships call in at Mahé from time to time.

All in all, political life in the Seychelles has the hallmarks of a Graham Greene novel with each of the major powers probably having 'a man in Victoria'.

The islands of the archipelago

The Seychelles consists of 115 islands of which only about 30 are inhabited. Although collectively constituting an area of a mere 175 square miles, the islands are scattered over about 515,000 square miles of the Indian Ocean.

The Seychelles are divided up into what are known as the Inner Islands and the Outer Islands. The predominantly granite-based Inner Islands make up about half of the land surface of the Seychelles, and include some of the largest of the islands, such as Mahé, Praslin, Silhouette, La Digue and Frégate. The distance from the cluster of Inner Islands to the Outer Islands located to the south-west varies from 62 miles to 677 miles. The Outer Islands are coral-based and are divided into three main clusters, the Amirantes Group, the Farquhar Group and the Aldabra Group. Apart from the island of Desroches in the Amirantes, none of the Outer Islands is readily accessible to tourists.

More than 90 per cent of the 70,000 Seychellois live on the main island of Mahé. Seventeen miles long and five miles wide, Mahé has the the widest range of scenic contrasts of all the islands – from its 68 gleaming white beaches to the exotic tropical forests and granite mountains that run down its spine. Mahé has the only

international airport in the Seychelles and has the only harbour capable of servicing ocean liners. The political and administrative capital, Victoria, is situated here, with about 30,000 people living in and around the town. Victoria ranks as one of the smallest capitals of the world – retaining an essentially village atmosphere and somewhat weathered charm.

Praslin, situated 17 miles to the north-west of Mahé is the second largest island in the group. It takes 15 minutes to get there by air from Mahé, or two hours by motor launch. About seven miles long and three miles wide, Praslin has about 5000 inhabitants who subsist mainly through agriculture, fishing and working in the various hotels on the island. One of the biggest attractions of the island is the Vallée de Mai, the national park which has recently been declared a World Heritage Site.

Third largest of the islands is Silhouette, lying 12 miles north-west of Mahé and easily visible from the latter's popular Beau Vallon beach. There are no roads to speak of, and it is only inhabited by about 250 people who farm and fish along its coast. It was supposedly once the home of Houdol, one of the most notorious pirates who plied the area. His treasure, the islanders swear, is still buried there.

The island of La Digue, located just two and a half miles east of Praslin, is, with its 2500 inhabitants, the third most populated of the islands. There are no tar roads and hardly any vehicles, the main forms of transportation being the ox cart and bicycle. Dotted along many of the island's beaches are huge, reddish granite boulders, interspersed with palm trees. Photographs of these spectacularly beautiful beaches appearing in guide books and travel posters have become the hallmark of the Seychelles.

Thirty-seven miles east of Mahé, 15 minutes journey by air, is the privately owned island of Frégate – a name synonymous in the Seychelles with lost pirate treasures. (A theory bolstered by intensive research done on old maps by Ian Fleming – the creator of James Bond.) Frégate is considered to have some of the most beautiful beaches in the Seychelles, and is densely covered with takamaka trees, casuarinas, mangoes, Indian almonds and breadfruit trees. A number of rare birds, such as the magpie robin, are found here, as well as scores of giant tortoises. There is only one hotel on the island, which is entered through the roots of a huge banyan tree.

Many things to many people

It's unlikely that any other group of islands in the Indian Ocean has preserved its natural heritage to the extent that Seychelles has done. The islands' rare and often unique flora (such as the insect-eating pitcher plant and the bizarre jellyfish tree) has made it a mecca for botanists; its spectacular coral reefs teeming with more than 1000 different species of fish have resulted in it becoming one of the world's number one venues for scuba divers; and the presence of large numbers of game fish out in the deeper waters – such as kingfish, sailfish, marlin and tuna – draw thousands of fishermen to these islands from the four corners of the globe. Combine these attractions with the delicious Creole cuisine served up on the island, a benevolent climate – the temperature rarely falls below 24°C (75°F) and seldom rises above 31°C (88°F) – and some of the world's most spectacularly beautiful beaches, and it is not hard to understand why the phrase 'island paradise' and Seychelles have become virtually synonymous.

The ubiquitous coconut palm, which grows almost everywhere on the islands, is the mainstay of the Seychelles' copra and coconut oil industry.

A Tropical Slice of France

Situated just above the Tropic of Capricorn, 500 miles to the east of Madagascar, the Indian Ocean island of Réunion is one of France's few remaining external territories – a reminder of centuries past when the French administered colonies dotted all over the world. But Réunion is by no means some forgotten outpost of another era – it remains as Gallic and vibrant as the *Marseillaise.* And as a holiday destination, this verdant island with its spectacular mountain scenery must rate as one of France's most carefully guarded secrets. Someone arriving on the island of Réunion for the first time is in for three very big surprises.

The first taste of the unexpected comes as you pass through the Gillot international air terminal and proceed along the seven-mile highway to Réunion's capital city, St Denis. This is, after all, just a relatively obscure little island in the Indian Ocean, with a population of just over 600,000 inhabitants – and yet you could be forgiven for imagining that you'd arrived in the heart of Europe. The airport is immaculately clean and briskly efficient; and multi-laned freeways and fly-overs hum with vehicles that look as though they've just been driven out of the showroom. Modern, stylish buildings and apartment blocks along the way help to complete the totally European impression.

The second surprise is just how utterly French the island is, and nowhere is this more evident than in St Denis – sometimes referred to as the 'Paris of the Indian Ocean'. Granted, the island is a French *département,* but one does not anticipate quite such a quintessentially Gallic flavour to things out here in the tropics, thousands of miles from France. Glitzy boutiques stock the very latest European fashions (and at Parisian prices!), and Pernod and pastis are sipped at sidewalk cafés amidst animated conversations.

Predictably, Peugeots, Citroëns and Renaults dominate the bustling streets of the capital, while neatly uniformed gendarmes keep a watchful eye on the swirl of activity around them. However, for those with little understanding of French, communicating can be a vexing problem. Most of the population speak only French or the local Creole dialect – English is more often than not greeted with a shrug of incomprehension.

The third revelation is the extraordinary landscape of the island. Volcanic in origin, Réunion is dominated by two separate mountain ranges which take up most of the island's surface. Driving from the coast towards the centre of the island one cannot help but be amazed at the dizzy presence of so many tortuous mountain passes, seemingly bottomless ravines and vertiginous

A row of cannons stand like wary sentinels behind the capital of St Denis. The island was lost by France only once – taken by the British in 1810 – but it was returned four years later in the terms of the Treaty of Paris.

peaks – the highest being the snow-capped Piton des Neiges (Snow Peak) that soars more than 10,000 feet above sea level. Again, the echo is of Europe, and the visitor has to remind himself yet again that he is traversing a small island only 128 miles in circumference, and not the Alps. There are pine trees aplenty, but the big giveaways are the ubiquitous aloes and assorted tropical fruit trees that cling to the mountain slopes.

Together with the nearby islands of Mauritius and Rodrigues, Réunion forms what is known as the Mascarene Archipelago, named after the Portuguese navigator, Pedro de Mascarenhas who discovered these islands in 1507. The first inhabitants of the island were a group of 12 mutineers from Madagascar who were exiled there by the island's governor in 1646. Their enforced stay on the island was obviously not too unpleasant, since on their return three years later they persuaded the governor to take over the island in the name of the King of France. It was initially named Ile Bourbon. In 1810 it was captured by the British but restored to France by the Treaty of Paris in 1814. It has been in French hands ever since.

Economic links with 'home'

Control of Réunion is expensive and some of the French argue that it brings their country little benefit or reward. The economy of Réunion is heavily reliant on its mother country, from where it imports about 60 per cent of its requirements and to where it exports about the same percentage of its products. The inflation rate on the island is, however, higher than that of France and unemployment is a growing problem.

The mainstay of the island's economy is agriculture, with about 70 per cent of the arable land devoted to the growing of sugar cane. Being a French territory, and therefore a part of the European Community, Réunion enjoys guaranteed markets and fixed prices for its sugar. Rum and cane spirit are also produced from the sugar cane molasses and marketed in France. In true French tradition, another important agricultural product in Réunion is essential oils for the perfume industry. The island is the world's biggest supplier of geranium oil; vetiver oil is also produced, albeit on a somewhat smaller scale. Other important crops include tobacco, vanilla and tropical fruits.

Tourism is also an important source of revenue. The majority of visitors – some 40,000 a year – are French, who take advantage of special cut-rate air fares to come over and enjoy the balmy climate of this tropical slice of France. But besides the regular stream of tourists from the mother country, the island – despite its immense charm – is not really part of the international tourist beat. This is probably because only 18 miles of its predominantly rocky coastline consists of beach, and the island is thus unable to compete on this score with nearby Mauritius, and the Seychelles farther north. But certainly some of the beaches along the west coast are attractive by any standards, offering safe bathing, good diving conditions and some excellent surfing locations. St-Gilles-les-Bains, with its 12-mile stretch of lagoon and white sand beach (many of Réunion's beaches consist of black, volcanic sand), is the island's principal seaside town.

Perhaps one of the island's biggest tourist drawcards is its mountainous interior. With its soaring peaks, mist-

The markets of Réunion offer a fascinating mélange of interesting characters and fascinating faces – such as this old man who is diligently shelling beans outside his store.

One of the highest points of habitation on Réunion is the town of Cilaos, which is 4000 feet above sea level at the centre of the island. It is particularly renowned for its fine, hand-embroidered linen.

filled river gorges, and precipitous paths connecting the two, Réunion is a haven for hikers and climbers. On weekends and holidays, busloads of people from the coastal towns head for the three *cirques* that dominate the interior of the island. There are ten *gîtes* (mountain lodges) dotted over this central, mountainous area for use as overnight stopovers, which have to be booked and paid for in advance.

backbone of the island's commercial life and administration. Amongst the Creoles and the whites, Roman Catholicism is the dominant religion. Twenty per cent of the population are Indians (known locally as the malabars) who consist mainly of Tamil Hindus. Their religious festivals add colour to the island's religious calendar. The balance of the population is Chinese (3 per cent) and Muslim (1 per cent).

Every shading under the sun

Réunion is something of a racial potpourri. The Creoles – descendants of African slaves, as well as the offspring of marriages between the races – are the largest ethnic group on the island, comprising about 40 per cent of the overall population. They are multi-hued people, varying in colour from ebony black through a spectrum of all shades of brown to ivory white. The red hair found in some can be traced back to Celtic settlers from Brittany and Normandy, and the wide range of facial features points to European, African, Indian and Chinese origins. French may be the official language of the island, but the language of the Creoles – originating in the earliest years of French colonisation – is the most widely spoken. Creole is fundamentally French with a simplified grammar, but using a more eclectic vocabulary in which French, Hindi, Arabic, Malgasy and English words are happily latched together.

Second to the Creoles in population are the whites, representing about 36 per cent of the population. Usually having strong ties with France, they form the

Réunion abounds with wonderful examples of colonial French architecture – in fact, the evolution of more than two centuries of Gallic architecture can be seen reflected in the diverse buildings on the island.

The palm-lined seafront park of Le Barachois at St Denis – the city's main gathering point. It is also a popular venue for games of boules – which is a favourite pastime for the people of Réunion.

The three *cirques*

Dominating the north-western interior of the island is a mountain range consisting of a cluster of three spectacular *cirques* – Cilaos, Salazie and Mafate. These *cirques* are the result of the original volcanoes that made up the range collapsing in on themselves to form *calderas*. Intensive erosion through the millenia has given them the shape of vast amphitheatres with crescent-shaped basins and precipitous cliffs.

The southernmost of the *cirques* is Cilaos (pronounced 'see-la-ross'). Cilaos is also the name of the main town of the area, which is situated in the middle of this *cirque*, 4000 feet above sea level. The town originated at the end of the 19th century as a colonial spa resort which utilised a hot spring in the area to treat rheumatism and other bone and muscular ailments; people from all over the island still go there to bathe in its supposedly therapeutic waters.

To the north-east of Cirque de Cilaos is Cirque de Salazie. It also had a thermal resort, situated at the little town of Hell-Bourg, but the spring there has dried up. Salazie is the most accessible of the three *cirques* and, with 7000 inhabitants is also the most populated. It is also the one most suited to agriculture, with crops of sugarcane, grapes, lemons, apples, peaches and tobacco.

The wildest and most visually impressive of the three *cirques* is Mafate. With no roads leading in, the sky above it is often abuzz with helicopters showing tourists the sights from an airborne vantage point. Despite its relative inaccessibility, Salazie is home to about 600 farmers who live on the small plateau within its rim. Because of its unspoilt character, Salazie is particularly popular as a hiking venue.

Botanical delights

Réunion's mountainous beauty is complemented by the lush vegetation that carpets its coastal areas, valleys and hillsides. Besides the palms, casuarinas and screw pines that are encountered everywhere, the island also has extensive forests of Japanese cryptomerieas, cabbage palms and tamarinds. Exotic flowers, such as jacarandas, bougainvilleas, hibiscuses and orchids, along with flowering trees and bushes – such as acacias and mimosa – all combine to make for a panoply of competing colours.

Réunion has a benevolent climate with temperatures along the coast seldom dropping below 20°C (68°F) in winter or rising above 30°C (86°F) in summer. The mountainous areas are cooler and less humid, with temperatures averaging 12°C (54°F) in winter and 18°C (64°F) in summer. Réunion falls within the cyclone belt, and during the cyclone season – from October to March – the inhabitants keep a wary eye on the weather. The last cyclone in 1987 resulted in millions of francs worth of damage.

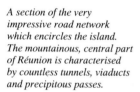

A section of the very impressive road network which encircles the island. The mountainous, central part of Réunion is characterised by countless tunnels, viaducts and precipitous passes.

Gazetteer

Africa

Covering more than 11 million square miles, Africa is, after
Asia, the world's second largest continent. It is nearly bisected
by the Equator, and both northern and southern Africa extend
to the mid-30s of latitude so that its climatic zones mirror each
other from the tropical forests of the equatorial region through
semitropical savannas, dry steppe lands and desert to the
Mediterranean climates of the extremities. More than 550
million people live in Africa, but it is lightly peopled, the
average density being less than 8 per square mile. The
birthrate is high, but is no longer matched by high death rates,
and the rate of population increase is rising sharply. For the
most part, the people are poor, and disease, famine and
drought are all too prevalent.

Most of Africa consists of high plateaus, which descend
steeply to generally narrow coastal regions. Waterfalls and
rapids flowing off the plateaus made exploration difficult, since
the only way into the continent for explorers was by sailing
upriver, and for long this contributed to the continent's
isolation. There are few natural harbours and the coastline is
very short in relation to the landmass; 14 out of the 47

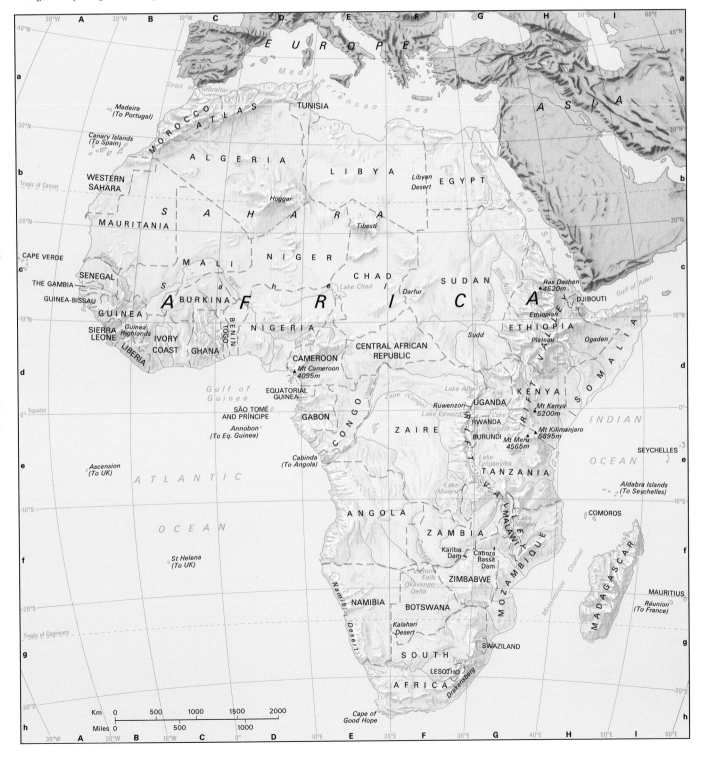

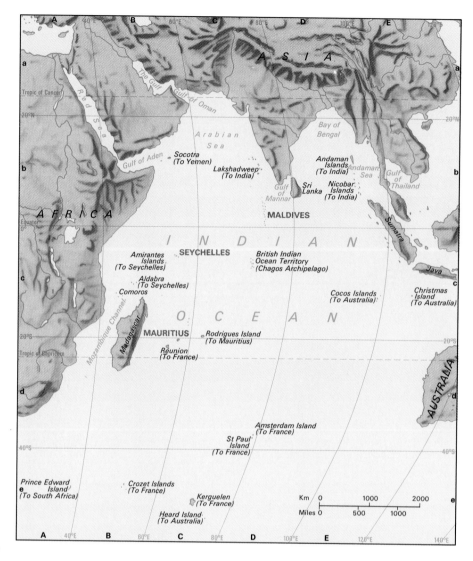

mainland African nations are landlocked. Four of the world's greatest rivers are in Africa: Nile, Zaire (Congo), Niger and Zambezi.

There are some majestic mountains, often made more so by their isolation in vast plains. In the north the Atlas range stretches 1400 miles from the Atlantic to Tunisia and reaches up to 13,671 feet at its highest point. In East Africa, the Ethiopian highlands form a great massif of intersecting ranges, whose loftiest peak is Ras Dashen (15,157 feet). Farther south along the East African Rift Valley are the Ruwenzori mountains, permanently snow-covered, and climbing to 16,765 feet, Mount Kenya (17,060 feet), Mount Meru (14,977 feet) and the mighty Kilimanjaro, Africa's highest mountain at 19,340 feet.

The East African Rift Valley, which is part of the Great Rift Valley system, is the world's most spectacular geological depression. It stretches from Beira in Mozambique in south-east Africa, and divides in two north of Lake Malawi. One branch runs north as far as Lake Albert (Mobutu), while the other, eastern branch becomes the trench of the Red Sea and continues into south-west Asia. Along the Rift Valley are some

of the world's largest lakes: Malawi (11,600 square miles), the 420-mile-long Tanganyika and the sea-like Victoria – 26,828 square miles.

Much of Central Africa is occupied by a great expanse of tropical rain forest, second in size only to that of the Amazon basin. It covers much of the coastlands of West Africa from The Gambia to Cameroon, and covers Gabon, Congo and half Zaire.

Nearly one-third of the continent is desert. The Sahara, the planet's largest arid area, alone covers 25 per cent of Africa – about 3 million square miles – while to the south are the Namib and Kalahari. Because of climatic changes and overgrazing, the Sahara is advancing some of its borders at an estimated 3 miles a year.

Africa is the hottest of the continents. Two-thirds of it is tropical or subtropical. The forests receive heavy rains that leach the soil, while other parts of the continent get less than 10 inches of rain a year. Devastating droughts are frequent. In 1983-5 both the north – especially Ethiopia – and also a great belt of land across the south of the continent suffered one of the most savage in history.

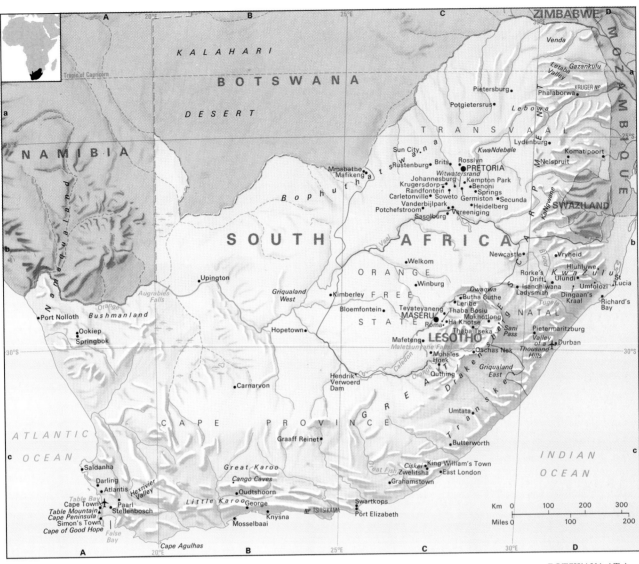

ANGOLA AT A GLANCE

Area 481,350 sq miles

Population 8,170,000

Capital Luanda

Government Marxist one-party state

Currency Kwanza = 100 lwei

Languages Portuguese (official) and Bantu languages

Religions Christian (70% Roman Catholic, 20% Protestant), tribal

Climate Tropical, with summer rains. Average temperatures in Luanda range from 18-23°C (64-73°F) in August to 24-30° C (75-86°F) in March

Main primary products Maize, cassava, bananas, palm oil, coffee, cotton, sisal, timber, fish; oil, diamonds, iron ore

Major industries Agriculture, mining, forestry, fishing, chemicals, tobacco, food processing

Main exports Crude oil and petroleum products, coffee, diamonds, sisal, palm oil, fish

Annual income per head (US$) 670

Population growth (per thous/yr) 27

Life expectancy (yrs) Male 41 **Female** 43

BENIN AT A GLANCE

Area 43,484 sq miles

Population 4,140 000

Capital Porto Novo (official), Cotonou (economic)

Government One-party republic

Currency CFA franc = 100 centimes

Languages French; also Fon, Yoruba and other African languages

Religions Animist (70%), Christian (15%), Muslim (13%)

Climate Tropical; average temperature in Cotonou ranges from 23°C (73°F) in August to 28°C (82°F) in March

Main primary products Cassava, yams, maize, sorghum, coffee, cotton, palm products, groundnuts

Major industries Agriculture, palm oil and palm-kernel oil processing, textiles, cotton ginning, beverages

Main exports Cotton, palm oil, palm kernels, cocoa (grown in Nigeria)

Annual imcome per head (US$) 260

Population growth (per thous/yr) 31

Life expectancy (yrs) Male 48 **Female** 52

BOTSWANA AT A GLANCE

Area 231,805 sq miles

Population 1,100,000

Capital Gaborone

Government Parliamentary republic

Currency Pula

Languages English (official) and Setswana

Religions Christian (15%), remainder tribal

Climate Subtropical and dry; average temperature in Francistown ranges from 5-23°C (41-73°F) in June to 18-31°C (64-88°F) in December/January

Main primary products Cattle, sheep, maize, sorghum; diamonds, nickel, copper

Major industries Cattle rearing, mining, meat processing, tourism

Main exports Diamonds, beef, nickel, copper

Annual income per head (US$) 930

Population growth (per thous/yr) 33

Life expectancy (yrs) Male 56 **Female** 62

BURKINA AT A GLANCE

Area 105,869 sq miles
Population 7,080,000
Capital Ouagadougou
Government One-party republic
Currency CFA franc = 100 centimes
Languages French (official), African languages
Religions Tribal religions (65%), Muslim (25%), Christian (10%)
Climate Tropical rains between May and November. Average temperature in Ouagadougou ranges from 16-33°C (61-91°F) in January to 26-39°C (79-102°F) in April
Main primary products Sorghum, millet, maize, rice, livestock, groundnuts, shea nuts, sesame, cotton
Major industries Agriculture, processed foods, textiles, mining, tyre manufacture
Main exports Cotton, livestock, sesame, groundnuts, shea-nut products, hides and skins, rubber tyres
Annual income per head (US$) 190
Population growth (per thous/yr) 25
Life expectancy (yrs) Male 43 **Female** 45

BURUNDI AT A GLANCE

Area 10,746 sq miles
Population 4,910,000
Capital Bujumbura
Government One-party republic
Currency Burundi franc = 100 centimes
Languages Kirundi, French, Swahili
Religions Christian (74%), tribal (20%), Muslim (6%)
Climate Equatorial; average temperature in Bujumbura 24°C (75°F)
Main primary products Cassava, sweet potatoes, maize, bananas, beans, coffee, tea, coconuts, cotton; nickel and uranium (both unexploited), tin
Major industries Agriculture, forestry, fishing, beverages
Main exports Coffee, tea, cotton
Annual income per head (US$) 255
Population growth (per thous/yr) 26
Life expectancy (yrs) Male 43 **Female** 47

CAMEROON AT A GLANCE

Area 183,570 sq miles
Population 10,035,000
Capital Yaoundé
Government One-party republic
Currency CFA franc = 100 centimes
Languages French and English (official), African languages
Religions Christian (33%), tribal (25%), Muslim (17%)
Climate Tropical; average temperature in Yaoundé ranges from 18°C (64°F) to 29°C (84°F)
Main primary products Maize, millet, yams, sorghum, cassava, plantains, cocoa, coffee, sweet potatoes, groundnuts, cotton, palm oil, livestock, timber, rubber; petroleum and natural gas, bauxite
Major industries Agriculture, mining, aluminium smelting, food processing, forestry, textiles
Main exports Petroleum, coffee, cocoa, timber, cotton, aluminium and rubber
Annual income per head (US$) 640
Population growth (per thous/year) 27
Life expectancy (yrs) Male 49 **Female** 52

CENTRAL AFRICAN REPUBLIC AT A GLANCE

Area 240,535 sq miles
Population 2,740,000
Capital Bangui
Government One-party military republic
Currency CFA franc = 100 centimes
Languages French (official), Sango
Religions Christian (35%), tribal religions (57%), Muslim (8%)
Climate Tropical; average temperature in Bangui ranges from 21-29°C (70-84°F) in July/August to 21-34°C (70-93°F) in February
Main primary products Cassava, groundnuts, bananas, plantains, sweet potatoes, maize, millet, coffee, cotton, timber; diamonds, gold, uranium (unexploited)
Major industries Agriculture, forestry, mining
Main exports Timber, coffee, diamonds, cotton, ivory, gold
Annual income per head (US$) 280
Population growth (per thous/yr) 28
Life expectancy (yrs) Male 42, **Female** 44

CHAD AT A GLANCE

Area 496,000 sq miles
Population 5,380,000
Capital N'djamena
Government One-party republic
Currency CFA franc = 100 centimes
Languages French, Arabic, African tribal languages
Religions Muslim (52%), Christian (5%), tribal religions (43%)
Climate Tropical; north arid to semiarid, wet season in south, May to October. Average temperature in N'djamena ranges from 14-33°C (57-91°F) in December to 23-42°C (73-108°F) in April
Main primary products Cotton, cattle, millet, sorghum, rice, cassava, fish; natron (sodium carbonate)
Major industries Agriculture, textiles, food processing, mining, fishing
Main exports Cotton, cattle, meat, processed fish
Annual income per head (US$) 100
Population growth (per thous/yr) 25
Life expectancy (yrs) male 42 **Female** 44

CONGO AT A GLANCE

Area 132,000 sq miles
Population 1,850,000
Capital Brazzaville
Government One-party Marxist republic
Currency CFA franc = 100 centimes
Languages French (official), local languages including Kongo, Lingala, Téké, Sanga
Religions Christian (50%), tribal religions (47%), Muslim (3%)
Climate Tropical; average temperature in Brazzaville ranges from 17-28°C (63-82°F) in July to 22-33°C (72-91°F) in April
Main primary products Cassava, sweet potatoes, groundnuts, pineapples, bananas, plantains, sugar cane, coffee, cocoa, timber; crude oil, lead, copper, zinc, gold
Major industries Crude oil production and refining, mining, forestry, food processing, textiles, cement, chemicals
Main exports Crude oil, timber and timber products, coffee, cocoa, diamonds (re-exports from Zaire)
Annual income per head (US$) 950
Population growth (per thous/yr) 30
Life expectancy (yrs) Male 58 **Female** 62

**EQUATORIAL GUINEA
AT A GLANCE**
Area 10,828 sq miles
Population 289,000
Capital Malabo
Government One-party
republic
Currency CFA franc = 100
centimes
Languages Spanish (official),
African languages including
Fang
Religions Christian (80%
Roman Catholic), tribal
Climate Tropical; average
temperature in Malabo ranges
from 21°C (70°F) to 32°C
(90°F)
Main primary products
Sweet potatoes, cassava,
bananas, coffee, cocoa,
coconuts, timber
Major industries Agriculture,
forestry, fishing, food
processing
Main exports Cocoa, timber,
coffee
**Annual income per head
(US$)** 140
**Population growth (per
thous/yr)** 25
Life expectancy (yrs) Male 43
Female 45

ETHIOPIA AT A GLANCE
Area 471,800 sq miles
Population 42,580,000
Capital Addis Ababa
Government Marxist military
republic
Currency Birr = 100 cents
Languages Amharic, Galla,
Sidamo, Arabic
Religions Muslim (45%),
Christian (40%), tribal (15%)
Climate Temperate on plateau,
hot in lowlands. Average
temperature in Addis Ababa
ranges from 5°C (41°F) to
25°C (77°F)
Main primary products
Wheat, barley, maize,
sorghum, millet, coffee,
cotton, sugar cane, beans and
peas, cattle, timber; salt
Major industries Agriculture,
food processing, textiles,
cement
Main exports Coffee, hides
and skins, beans, cotton,
sesame seeds
**Annual income per head
(US$)** 126
**Population growth (per
thous/yr)** 7
Life expectancy (yrs) Male 39,
Female 43

GABON AT A GLANCE
Area 103,346 sq miles
Population 1,020,000
Capital Libreville
Government One-party
republic
Currency CFA franc = 100
centimes
Languages French (official),
Bantu languages
Religions Christianity (50%),
rest mainly tribal, with 2000
Muslims
Climate Equatorial; average
temperature in Libreville
ranges from 24°C (75°F) to
27°C (81°F)
Main primary products
Cocoa, coffee, palm oil,
bananas, sugar cane, cassava,
plantains, maize, rice,
livestock, timber, petroleum
manganese, uranium, iron ore
Major industries Mining,
petroleum production and
refining, agriculture, forestry,
fishing, food processing
Main exports Petroleum,
manganese, uranium, timber
**Annual income per head
(US$)** 3040
**Population growth (per
thous/yr)** 31
Life expectancy (yrs) Male 47
Female 51

**THE GAMBIA AT A
GLANCE**
Area 4,361 sq miles
Population 777,000
Capital Banjul (formerly
called Bathurst)
Government Parliamentary
republic
Currency Dalasi = 100 bututs
Languages English (official),
African languages
Religions Muslim (85%),
tribal, Christian
Climate Tropical; temperature
in Banjul ranges from 15-31°C
(59-88°F) in January, 23-32°C
(73-90°F) in June
Main primary products
Groundnuts, cassava, millet,
rice, cattle, fish, timber, palm
kernels
Major industries Agriculture,
food processing, fishing,
forestry
Main exports Groundnuts and
derived products, fish, hides
and skins
**Annual income per head
(US$)** 350
**Population growth (per
thous/yr)** 35
Life expectancy (yrs) Male 35
Female 37

GHANA AT A GLANCE
Area 92,099 sq miles
Population 13,590,000
Capital Accra
Government Republic
military-civilian junta
Currency Cedi = 100 pesewas
Languages English (official),
Akan, Ga, Ewe
Religions Christian (42%),
tribal (38%), Muslim (12%)
Climate Tropical; average
temperature in Accra ranges
from 22°C (72°F) to 31°C
(88°F)
Main primary products
Cassava, taro, maize, yams,
bananas, cocoa, sorghum,
timber; gold, diamonds,
manganese, bauxite
Major industries Agriculture,
bauxite refining, steel, oil
refining, food processing,
cement, vehicle assembly,
forestry, mining
Main exports Cocoa, gold,
timber, diamonds, manganese
ore, bauxite and alumina
**Annual income per head
(US$)** 370
**Population growth (per
thous/yr)** 30
Life expectancy (yrs) Male 53
Female 56

GUINEA AT A GLANCE
Area 94,926 sq miles
Population 5,890,000
Capital Conakry
Government Military-
dominated republic
Currency Guinean franc
Languages French (official),
eight official local languages
Religions Muslim (69%),
tribal religions (30%),
Christian (1%)
Climate Tropical; wet season
from May to November.
Average temperature in
Conakry ranges from 22°C
(72°F) to 32°C (90°F)
Main primary products Rice,
maize, cassava, bananas;
bauxite, iron ore, diamonds
Major industries Agriculture,
mining, bauxite refining,
fishing
Main exports Bauxite,
alumina, diamonds
**Annual income per head
(US$)** 290
**Population growth (per
thous/yr)** 27
Life expectancy (yrs) Male 42
Female 44

GUINEA-BISSAU AT A GLANCE

Area 13,948 sq miles
Population 874,000
Capital Bissau
Government Military-dominated republic
Currency Peso = 100 centavos
Languages Portuguese, Criolo (Creole), African languages
Religions Tribal (65%), Muslim (30%), Christian (5%)
Climate Tropical; heavy rains June to November; average temperature ranges from 24 to 27°C (75 to 81°F)
Main primary products Cereals, coconuts, groundnuts, rice, palm kernels, timber, fish; bauxite
Major industries Agriculture, fishing, forestry, beverages
Main exports Fish, groundnuts, palm kernels, timber
Annual income per head (US$) 180
Population growth (per thous/yr) 19
Life expectancy (yrs) Male 39 **Female** 43

IVORY COAST AT A GLANCE

Area 124,503 sq miles
Population 10,460,000
Capital Yamoussoukro
Government One-party republic
Currency CFA franc = 100 centimes
Languages French and tribal languages
Religions Animist (63%), Christian (12%), Muslim (23%)
Climate Tropical; average temperature in Abidjan ranges from 22°C (72°C) to 32°C (90°F)
Main primary products Cocoa, coffee, cotton, bananas, pineapples, rubber, sugar, rice, cassava, yams, timber; crude oil, diamonds, cobalt, uranium
Major industries Agriculture, food processing, textiles, leather goods, forestry, mining, petroleum refining
Main exports Cocoa, coffee, timber, petroleum products, cotton
Annual income per head (US$) 1030
Population growth (per thous/yr) 40
Life expectancy (yrs) Male 46 **Female** 48

KENYA AT A GLANCE

Area 224,960 sq miles
Population 21,040,000
Capital Nairobi
Government One-party republic
Currency Kenya shilling = 100 cents
Languages Swahili, English, tribal languages
Religions Christian (66%), tribal religions (26%), Muslim (6%)
Climate Tropical; hot and humid on coast, temperate inland, dry to the north. Average temperatures in Nairobi range from 11-21°C (52-70°F) in July to 13-26°C (55-79°F) in February
Main primary products Maize, millet, beans, cassava, potatoes, sweet potatoes, sugar, coffee, tea, cotton, sisal, cattle, pyrethrum (flower used in insecticides)
Major industries Agriculture, oil refining, cement, food processing, tourism
Main exports Coffee, tea, petroleum products, fruit and vegetables, sugar, chemicals, cement, hides and skins
Annual income per head (US$) 315
Population growth (per thous/yr) 42
Life expectancy (yrs) Male 54 **Female** 58

LESOTHO AT A GLANCE

Area 11,720 sq miles
Population 1,550,000
Capital Maseru
Government Parliamentary monarchy
Currency Loti = 100 lisente
Languages Sesotho, English
Religions Christian (80%), tribal religions (20%)
Climate Continental; temperature in Maseru ranges from -3 to 17°C (27-63°F) in July to 15-33°C (59-91°F) in January
Main primary products Wheat, maize sorghum, pulses, livestock; diamonds
Major industries Agriculture, tourism
Main exports Wool, mohair, diamonds
Annual income per head (US$) 370
Population growth (per thous/yr) 25
Life expectancy (yrs) Male 51 **Female** 54

LIBERIA AT A GLANCE

Area 43, 000 sq miles
Population 2,300,000
Capital Monrovia
Government Military-ruled republic
Currency Liberian dollar = 100 cents, US dollar also used
Languages English, local languages
Religions Tribal (75%), Christian (10%), Muslim (15%)
Climate Tropical; average temperature in Monrovia ranges from 22°C (72°F) to 31°C (88°F)
Main primary products Rice, cassava, bananas, rubber, palm kernels, maize, coffee, cocoa, timber; iron ore, gold, diamonds
Major industries Mining, forestry, agriculture
Main exports Iron ore, rubber, timber, diamonds, coffee, gold, cocoa
Annual income per head (US$) 360
Population growth (per thous/yr) 33
Life expectancy (yrs) Male 52 **Female** 55

MADAGASCAR AT A GLANCE

Area 226,657 sq miles
Population 10,200, 000
Capital Antananarivo
Government Marxist republic
Currency Madagascar franc = 100 centimes
Languages Malagasy (official), French
Religions Tribal religions (50%), Christian (40%), Muslim (7%)
Climate Tropical; cooler at altitude. Temperatures in Antananarivo 9-20°C (48-68°F) in July; 16-27°C (61-81°F) in December
Main primary products Rice, cassava, mangoes, vanilla, bananas, potatoes, sugar cane, maize, coffee, pepper, cattle, timber; graphite, chromium, zircon, beryl, garnet
Major industries Agriculture, oil refining, forestry, food processing, mining
Main exports Coffee, vanilla, cloves, petroleum products, meat, fish, sugar
Annual income per head (US$) 300
Population growth (per thous/yr) 28
Life expectancy (yrs) Male 46 **Female** 49

MALAWI AT A GLANCE
Area 45,747 sq miles
Population 7,290,000
Capital Lilongwe
Government One-party republic
Currency Kwacha = 100 tambala
Languages Chichewa, English
Religions Christian (60%), tribal religions (20%), Muslim (16%)
Climate Tropical; cooler in the highlands. Average temperature ranges from 14-24°C (57-75°F) between November and April to 19-32°C (66-90°F) May to October
Main primary products Maize, rice, cassava, sorghum, millet, beans, groundnuts, sugar, tea, tobacco, cotton
Major industries Agriculture, food processing, brewing, cement, tourism
Main exports Tobacco, sugar, tea, groundnuts, cotton, textiles, cereals
Annual income per head (US$) 190
Population growth (per thous/yr) 33
Life expectancy (yrs) Male 43 **Female** 45

MALI AT A GLANCE
Area 478,767 sq miles
Population 7,910,000
Capital Bamako
Government One-party republic under military rule
Currency CFA franc = 100 centimes
Languages French (official), Bambara, Fulani, Mandingo
Religions Muslim (90%), Animist (9%), Christian (1%)
Climate Hot and dry; temperatures at Bamako range from 16-33°C (61-91°F) in January to 24-39°C (75-102°F) in April
Main primary products Millet, maize, vegetables, rice, groundnuts, cotton, sorghum, sugar cane, livestock, fish
Major industries Agriculture, processed foods, tanning, fishing
Main exports Cotton, livestock (cattle), groundnuts, rice
Annual income per head (US$) 170
Population growth (per thous/yr) 23
Life expectancy (yrs) Male 43, **Female** 46

MAURITANIA AT A GLANCE
Area 397,953 sq miles
Population 1,690,000
Capital Nouakchott
Government Military
Currency Ouguiya = 5 khoums
Languages Arabic, French (official), African languages
Religions Muslim
Climate Hot and dry, summer rains near coast. Average temperature in Nouakchott ranges from 13-28°C (55-82°F) in December to 24-34°C (75-93°F) in September
Main primary products Livestock, millet, sorghum, dates, fish; iron ore, copper, phosphates, salt
Major industries Agriculture, mining, fishing
Main exports Iron ore, processed fish
Annual income per head (US$) 400
Population growth (per thous/yr) 20
Life expectancy (yrs) Male 43 **Female** 46

MAURITIUS AT A GLANCE
Area 720 sq miles (excluding Rodrigues and dependencies)
Population 1,020,000
Capital Port Louis
Government Parliamentary monarchy
Currency Mauritius rupee = 100 cents
Languages English, French, Creole, Hindi
Religions Roman Catholic, Hindu, Muslim
Climate Subtropical; average temperature ranges from 17-24°C (63-75°F) in August to 23-30°C (73-86°F) in January
Main primary products Sugar cane, tea, tobacco, potatoes
Major industries Agriculture, sugar processing, molasses, rum distilling, textiles, clothing, fertilisers, electronic equipment, tourism
Main exports Sugar, molasses, rum, clothing, textile yarns and fabrics
Annual income per head (US$) 1050
Population growth (per thous/yr) 9
Life expectancy (yrs) Male 64 **Female** 68

MOZAMBIQUE AT A GLANCE
Area 308,642 sq miles
Population 14,160,000
Capital Maputo
Government One-party (Marxist) republic
Currency Metical = 100 centavos
Languages Portuguese (official), Bantu languages
Religions Animist (60%), Christian (18%), Muslim (16%)
Climate Humid, tropical; dry season from June to September. Temperatures in Maputo range from 13-24°C (55-75°F) in July to 22-31°C (72-88°F) in February
Main primary products Cotton, cashew nuts, tea, sugar, cassava, cereals, bananas, sisal, groundnuts, coconuts; coal
Major industries Agriculture, textiles, chemicals, food processing, petroleum products, cement, mining
Main exports Cashew nuts, textiles, tea, cotton
Annual income per head (US$) 159
Population growth (per thous/yr) 28
Life expectancy (yrs) Male 47 **Female** 50

NAMIBIA AT A GLANCE
Area 317,827 sq miles excluding Walvis Bay
Population 1,140,000
Capital Windhoek
Government Administered by South Africa
Currency South African rand = 100 cents
Languages English and Afrikaans (official), German and several Bantu
Religions Christian (90%), remainder tribal
Climate Temperate and subtropical, very dry; temperatures in Windhoek range from 6-20°C (43-68°F) in July to 17-29° C (63-84°F) in January
Main primary products Cattle, sheep, maize, millet, sorghum, fish; diamonds, copper, lead, zinc, tin, uranium, vanadium
Major industries Mining, stock rearing, food processing, textiles, ore smelting, fishing
Main exports Diamonds, copper, lead, zinc, uranium, fish, cattle, karakul fur pelts
Annual income per head (US$) 1800
Population growth (per thous/yr) 30
Life expectancy (yrs) Male 50 **Female** 53

NIGER AT A GLANCE
Area 489,191 sq miles
Population 6,700,000
Capital Niamey
Government Military republic
Currency CFA franc = 100 centimes
Languages French (official), Hausa and other local languages
Religions Muslim (85%), Animist (14%), Christian (0.5%)
Climate Hot and dry; average temperature in Niamey ranges from 14-34°C (57-93°F) in January to 27-41°C (81-106°F) in May
Main primary products Millet, sorghum, groundnuts, cotton, rice, livestock; uranium, tin; phosphates
Major industries Agriculture, textiles, food processing, mining
Main exports Uranium, groundnuts, livestock, hides and skins
Annual income per head (US$) 300
Population growth (per thous/yr) 33
Life expectancy (yrs) Male 43 **Female** 46

NIGERIA AT A GLANCE
Area 356,669 sq miles
Population 94,300,000
Capital Lagos
Government Federal republic under military rule
Currency Naira + 100 kobo
Languages English (official), Hausa, Ibo, Yoruba
Religions Muslim (48%), Christian (35%), tribal
Climate Tropical; wettest month June. Average temperature ranges from 23°C (73°F) to 32°C (90°F)
Main primary products Groundnuts, cotton, cocoa, rubber, maize, millet, sorghum, cassava, rice, yams, palm kernels, livestock, timber; oil and natural gas, tin, coal, iron ore
Major industries Oil and natural gas production and refining, agriculture, mining, petrochemicals, fertilisers, motor vehicles, cement, food processing
Main exports Crude oil and refined products, natural gas, cocoa, tin, timber and hides
Annual income per head (US$) 740
Population growth (per thous/yr) 34
Life expectancy (yrs) Male 48 **Female** 51

RWANDA AT A GLANCE
Area 10,169 sq miles
Population 6,480,000
Capital Kigali
Government Military-ruled republic
Currency Rwanda franc = 100 centimes
Languages Kinyarwanda, French, Kiswahili
Religions Christian (65%), tribal religions (25%), Muslim (10%)
Climate Tropical; modified by altitude; average annual temperature in Kigali is 19°C (66°F)
Main primary products Sweet potatoes, cassava, potatoes, beans and peas, sorghum, bananas, groundnuts, coffee, tea, pyrethrum, cattle, sheep, goats, pigs, timber; tin, tungsten
Major industries Agriculture, mining, forestry, processing hides and skins, food processing
Main exports Coffee, metal ores, tea, hides and skins, pyrethrum
Annual income per head (US$) 250
Population growth (per thous/yr) 37
Life expectancy (yrs) Male 44 **Female** 47

SENEGAL AT A GLANCE
Area 75,750 sq miles
Population 6,971,200
Capital Dakar
Government Parliamentary republic
Currency CFA franc = 100 centimes
Languages French (official), African languages – mainly Wolof
Religions Muslim (90%), Christian (6%), tribal religions (3%)
Climate Tropical; average temperature in Dakar ranges from 18-26°C (64-79°F) in January to 24-32°C (75-90°F) in September
Main primary products Rice, millet, sorghum, maize, groundnuts, fish, timber; phosphates
Major industries Agriculture, petroleum refining, phosphate fertiliser manufacture, textiles, beverages, fishing, forestry, cement and processed food
Main exports Petroleum products, fish, phosphate fertiliser, cotton fabrics, groundnut oil
Annual income per head (US$) 410
Population growth (per thous/yr) 32
Life expectancy (yrs) Male 43 **Female** 45

SEYCHELLES AT A GLANCE
Area 175 sq miles
Population 66,000
Capital Victoria (on Mahé)
Government One-party republic
Currency Seychelles rupee = 100 cents
Languages Creole, French, English
Religion Christian (90% Roman Catholic, 8% Anglican)
Climate Tropical; average temperature 26°C (79°F)
Main primary products Fish, fruit, vegetables, coconuts
Major industries Tourism, fishing, brewing, cigarette manufacture
Main exports Fish, copra, cinnamon bark, fertiliser (guano)
Annual income per head (US$) 2300
Population growth (per thous/yr) 9
Life expectancy (yrs) Male 65, **Female** 71

SIERRA LEONE AT A GLANCE
Area 27,691 sq miles
Population 3,980,000
Capital Freetown
Government Parliamentary republic
Currency Leone = 100 cents
Languages English (official), Krio, Mende, Temne and other local languages
Religions Animist, Muslim, Christian
Climate Tropical; average temperature in Freetown 23-31°C (73-88°F)
Main primary products Rice, cassava, groundnuts, coffee, cocoa, timber, palm nuts, fish; diamonds, bauxite, iron ore
Major industries Agriculture, mining, fishing, forestry
Main exports Diamonds, bauxite, coffee, cocoa, iron ore, palm kernels
Annual income per head (US$) 280
Population growth (per thous/yr) 26
Life expectancy (yrs) Male 46 **Female** 49

SOMALIA AT A GLANCE
Area 246,199 sq miles
Population 7,822,900
Capital Mogadishu
Government One-party republic
Currency Somali shilling
Language Somali
Religion Muslim
Climate Hot and dry. Average temperature in Mogadishu ranges from 23°C (73°F) to 32°C (90°F)
Main primary products Sheep, goats, camels, bananas, sugar cane, cotton, maize, millet
Major industries Stock-rearing and small-scale textiles, sugar refining, flour milling
Main exports Meat, hides and skins, livestock, bananas
Annual income per head (US$) 220
Population growth (per thous/yr) 30
Life expectancy (yrs) Male 39, **Female** 39

SOUTH AFRICA AT A GLANCE
Area 471,445 sq miles including black homelands
Population 33,340,000 including black homelands
Capital Pretoria (administrative)
Government Parliamentary republic
Currency Rand = 100 cents
Languages English (official), Afrikaans and Bantu languages especially Zulu and Xhosa
Religions Christian (70%), Bantu churches (26%), Hindu (2%), Muslim (1%), Jewish (1%)
Climate Temperate warm and sunny. Average temperature in Cape Town ranges from 9 - 17°C (48-63°F) in July to 16-27°C (61-81°F) in February
Main primary products Cereals, sugar, grapes, livestock, potatoes, citrus fruits, apples, pineapples, tobacco, cotton, timber, fish; gold, coal, iron ore, diamonds, copper, manganese, limestone, chrome, silver, nickel, phosphates, asbestos, tin, zinc, vermiculite
Major industries Iron and steel, mining, food processing, motor vehicles, mineral-refining machinery, chemicals, petroleum refining, agriculture, tobacco products, clothing, paper, textiles, forestry, fishing
Main exports Gold, food, coal, iron and steel, diamonds, gold coins, metal ores
Annual income per head (US$) 1870
Populaton growth (per thous/yr) 27
Life expectancy (yrs) Male 61 **Female** 65

SUDAN AT A GLANCE
Area 967,500 sq miles
Population 22,350,000
Capital Khartoum
Government Republic
Currency Sudanese pound = 100 piastres = 1000 milliemes
Languages Arabic, English, local languages especially Nubian
Religions Muslim (73%), tribal (18%), Christian (9%)
Climate Tropical; average temperature in Khartoum ranges from 15-32°C (59-90°F) in January to 26-41°C (79-106°F) in June
Main primary products Cotton, dates, groundnuts, sesame seeds, gum arabic, sorghum, wheat, beans, livestock; crude oil and natural gas, chromium
Major industries Agriculture, oil production and refining, food processing, cement
Main exports cotton, sesame seed, groundnuts, cereals, gum arabic, livestock, petroleum products
Annual income per head (US$) 390
Population growth (per thous/yr) 27
Life expectancy (yrs) Male 45, **Female** 48

SWAZILAND AT A GLANCE
Area 6,705 sq miles
Population 691,000
Capital Mbabane
Government Absolute monarchy
Currency Lilangeni = 100 cents
Languages English, siSwati (Swazi)
Religions Christian (70%), traditional religions (30%)
Climate Subtropical moderated by altitude; average temperature in Mbabane ranges from 6-17°C (43-63°F) in June to 15-25°C (59-77°F) in January/February
Main primary products Maize, cotton, rice, sugar, citrus fruits, tobacco, cattle, timber; asbestos, coal
Major industries Agriculture, forestry, mining, timber processing, chemicals, tourism
Main exports Sugar, wood pulp, chemicals, asbestos, citrus fruits
Annual income per head (US$) 740
Population growth (per thous/yr) 30
Life expectancy (yrs) Male 51 **Female** 56

TANZANIA AT A GLANCE
Area 364, 886 sq miles
Population 22,430,000
Capital Dar es Salaam effectively, though due to be replaced by Dodoma
Government One-party socialist republic
Currency Tanzanian shilling = 100 cents
Languages Swahili (official), English
Religions Christianity (40%), Islam (23%), tribal religions (23%), Hinduism (4%)
Climate Hot and humid coast; dry inland with temperatures governed by altitude. Average temperature in Dar es Salaam ranges from 19°C (66°F) to 31°C (88°F)
Main primary products Maize, cotton, coffee, sisal, cloves, coconuts, tobacco, cassava, beans; diamonds
Major industries Agriculture, food processing, textiles, cement, oil refining
Main exports Cotton, coffee, cloves, coconut products, diamonds, sisal
Annual income per head (US$) 270
Population growth (per thous/yr) 32
Life expectancy (yrs) Male 50 **Female** 53

TOGO AT A GLANCE
Area 21,925 sq miles
Population 3,110,000
Capital Lomé
Government One-party republic
Currency CFA franc = 100 centimes
Languages French (official), Ewe, Kabra and other local languages
Religions Tribal (50%), Christian (27%), Muslim (12%)
Climate Tropical; average annual temperature in Lomé 27°C (81°F)
Main primary products Cassava, maize, millet, oil palms, groundnuts, cotton, cocoa, coffee, livestock; phosphates
Major industries Mining, cement, agriculture, textiles, food processing
Main exports Phosphates, cocoa, coffee
Annual income per head (US$) 280
Population growth (per thous/yr) 31
Life expectancy (yrs) Male 46 **Female** 50

UGANDA AT A GLANCE
Area 91,344 sq miles
Population 15,200,000
Capital Kampala
Government Republic
Currency Uganda shilling = 100 cents
Languages English (official), Swahili, Bantu and Luganda languages
Religions Christian (65%), Muslim (10%)
Climate Equatorial, tropical; cooler in mountain areas. Temperature ranges from 15°C (59°F) to 26°C (79°F)
Main primary products Coffee, cotton, tea, sugar, livestock, millet, maize, bananas, sorghum, yams, timber; copper, phosphates
Major industries Agriculture, food processing, textiles, cement, copper processing, motor vehicles, metal processing, mining
Main exports Coffee, cotton, tea
Annual income per head (US$) 180
Population growth (per thous/yr) 32
Life expectancy (yrs) Male 46, **Female** 49

ZAIRE AT A GLANCE
Area 905,360 sq miles
Population 33,940,000
Capital Kinshasa
Government One-party republic
Currency Zaire = 100 makuta
Languages French (official), Lingala, Swahili, Kikongo, Tshiluba
Religions Tribal (50%), Christian (45%), Muslim (1%)
Climate Tropical, equatorial in centre; average temperature in Kinshasa ranges from 18°C (64°F) to 32°C (90°F)
Main primary products Cassava, plantains, maize, sugar cane, groundnuts, bananas, palm oil and kernels, coffee, rubber, cotton, cocoa, tea, timber; copper, oil and natural gas, cobalt, zinc, tin, diamonds, gold
Major industries Agriculture, foodstuffs, oil refining, textiles, clothing, mining, forestry
Main exports Copper, cobalt, coffee, diamonds
Annual income per head (US$) 160
Population growth (per thous/yr) 29
Life expectancy (yrs) Male 48 **Female** 52

ZAMBIA AT A GLANCE
Area 290, 586 sq miles
Population 6,990,000
Capital Lusaka
Government One-party republic
Currency Kwacha = 100 ngwe
Languages English (official), Bemba, Nyanja, Lozi, Tonga and other local languages
Religions Christian (65%), tribal (30%)
Climate Tropical; cool in the highlands. Average temperature in Lusaka ranges from 9-23°C (48-73°F) in July to 18-31°C (64-88°F) in October
Main primary products Maize, cassava, sugar, tobacco, cotton, groundnuts, beef cattle, copper, cobalt, zinc, lead, coal
Major industries Agriculture, mining, brewing, chemicals, cement
Main exports Copper, cobalt, zinc, lead
Annual income per head (US$) 430
Population growth (per thous/yr) 32
Life expectancy (yrs) Male 49 **Female** 52

ZIMBABWE AT A GLANCE
Area 150,810 sq miles
Population 8,950,000
Capital Harare (formerly called Salisbury)
Government Parliamentary republic
Currency Zimbabwe dollar = 100 cents
Languages English (official), Shona, Ndebele
Religions Christian (55%), tribal (40%), Muslim (1%)
Climate Subtropical; average temperature in Harare ranges from 7-21°C (45-70°F) in June/July to 16-27°C (61-81°F) in November
Main primary products Maize, tobacco, wheat, sugar, millet, cotton; gold, asbestos, coal, iron, chrome, nickel, copper, tin
Major industries Agriculture, cigarettes, fertilisers, cement, coke, iron and steel, textiles, mining, tourism
Main exports Tobacco, foodstuffs, ferro-chrome, gold, asbestos, cotton
Annual income per head (US$) 860
Population growth (per thous/yr) 33
Life expectancy (yrs) Male 53 **Female** 57

Picture Credits

p.9 Mark van Aardt Photographic Enterprises; p.10 top Gerald Cubitt; bottom Anthony Bannister Photo Library; p.11 Gerald Cubitt; p.12 Shawn Benjamin; p.12/13 Anthony Bannister Photo Library; p.13 The Argus; p.14 left Peter Ribton; right Peter Ribton; p.15 top Walter Knirr; bottom Jean Morris; p.16 Jean Morris; p.17 top left Walter Knirr; top right Photo Access; bottom The Argus Company; p.18 left Walter Knirr; right Walter Knirr; p.19 top Anna Zieminski; bottom Shawn Benjamin; p.20/1 Anthony Bannister Photo Library; p.21 Walter Knirr; p.22 left Shawn Benjamin; right Shawn Benjamin; p.23 John Paisley-Photo Access; p.24 Walter Knirr; p.24/5 Walter Knirr; p.26 top Roger de la Harpe; bottom Anthony Bannister Photo Library; p.27 Gerald Cubitt; p.28 Anthony Bannister Photo Library; p.29 top Gerald Cubitt; bottom Jean Morris; p.30 Walter Knirr; p.31 top Mark van Aardt Photographic Enterprises; bottom Mark van Aardt Photographic Enterprises; p.32 left Mark van Aardt Photographic Enterprises; right Photo Access; p.32/3 Mark van Aardt Photographic Enterprises; p.33 Photo Access; p.34 Shawn Benjamin; p.34/5 Anthony Bannister Photo Library; p.35 top Shaen Adey; bottom Walter Knirr; p.36 top Gill Bunce; bottom Shaen Adey; p.37 top Walter Knirr; bottom David Briers; p.38 top Anthony Bannister Photo Library; bottom Anthony Bannister Photo Library; p.39 Anthony Bannister Photo Library; p.40 David Steele; p.40/1 Walter Knirr; p.41 Gerald Cubitt; p.42 top Photo Access; bottom left Shawn Benjamin; bottom right Photo Access; p.43 top Walter Knirr; bottom Anthony Bannister Photo Library; p.44 Mark van Aardt Photographic Enterprises; p.45 left Gerald Cubitt; right Mark van Aardt Photographic Enterprises; p.46 top Mark van Aardt Photographic Enterprises; bottom Anthony Bannister Photo Library; p.47 top Photo Access; bottom Anthony Bannister Photo Library; p.48 left Jean Morris; right

Anthony Bannister Photo Library; p.49 top Photo Access; bottom Anthony Bannister Photo Library; p.50 Walter Knirr; p.51 top Walter Knirr; bottom Mark van Aardt Photographic Enterprises; right Photo Access; p.52 left Jean Morris; right Jean Morris; p.53 Mark van Aardt Photographic Enterprises; p.54 Roger de la Harpe; p.54/5 Shaen Adey; p.55 Shaen Adey; p.56 Roger de la Harpe; p.56/7 Shaen Adey; p.57 Walter Knirr; p.58 left Walter Knirr; right Jean Morris; p.59 Walter Knirr; p.60 Anthony Bannister Photo Library; p.60/1 Mark van Aardt Photographic Enterprises; p.61 David Briers; p.62 top Mark van Aardt Photographic Enterprises; bottom left Shawn Benjamin; bottom right Shawn Benjamin; p.63 Mark van Aardt Photographic Enterprises; p.64 left Gerald Cubitt; right Jean Morris. p.64/5 Mark van Aardt Photographic Enterprises; p.65 Jean Morris; left Walter Knirr; right Anthony Bannister Photo Library; p.66/7 Mark van Aardt Photographic Enterprises; p.67 Photo Access; p.68 Walter Knirr; p.69 Seed-Rapho; p.70 top Pix, bottom Kérébel-Diaf; p.71 Rafi-Leda; p.72 Planchard-Pix; p.73 top S.Held, bottom S.Held; p.74 Trigalou-Pix; p.75 J.Bottin; p.76 Huet-Hoa Qui; p.77 Gasquet-Hoa Qui; p.78 C.Lénars; p.79 top Basi-Sore-Hoa Qui, bottom Duchêne-Diaf; p.80 top Revault-Pix, bottom Camerapix-A. Hutchison Lby; p.81 Camerapix-A.Hutchison Lby; p.82 Charliat-Rapho; p.83 C.Lénars; p.84 left Grandadam-Explorer, right C.Lénars; p.85 J.Bottin; p.86 top Boutin-Explorer, bottom Duchêne-Diaf; p.87 Camerapix-A.Hutchison Lby; p.88 Pratt-Pries-Diaf; p.89 Gerster-Rapho; p.90 Boutin-Explorer; p.91 top S.Held, bottom S.Held; p.92 S.Held; p.93 top S.Held, bottom Valentin-Explorer; p.94 Pinheira-Top; p.95 J.Bottin, p.96 Camerapix-A.Hutchison Lby; p.97 Marenthier-Hoa Qui; p.98 top Pinheira-Top, bottom Schoenahl-Diaf; p.99 Pinheira-Top; p.100

Pinheira-Top; p.101 Pinheira-Top; p.102 top C.Lénars, bottom Pinheira-Top; p.103 B.Régent-Diaf; p.104 Mallet-Explorer; p.105 top C.Lénars, bottom Camerapix-A. Hutchison Lby; p.106 Vuillomenet-Rapho; p.107 top Huet-Hoa Qui, bottom Boutin-Explorer; p.108 Marenthier-Hoa Qui; p.109 C.Lénars; p.110 top J.Bottin, bottom Kérébel-Diaf; p.111 J.Bottin; p.112 Arthus-Bertrand-Explorer; p.113 top J.Bottin, bottom S.Held; p.114 Arthus-Bertrand-Explorer; p.115 C.Lénars; p.116 left Orivel-Hoa Qui, right Orivel-Hoa Qui; p.117 Gabanou-Diaf; p.118 top J.Bottin, bottom Pavard-Hoa Qui; p.119 Huet-Hoa qui; p.120 Barbier-Diaf; p.121 Gabanou-Diaf; p.122 left Richer-Hoa Qui, right Richer-Hoa Qui; p.123 S.Held; p.124 J.L-Peyromaure; p.125 Armand-Photothèque-S.D.P; p.126 J.L-Peyromaure; p.127 top J.L-Peyromaure, bottom Edouard-Photothèque-S.D.P; p.128 Pix; p.129 Vincent Leroux; p.130 top Vincent Leroux; bottom Vincent Leroux; p.131 Vincent Leroux; p.132 Vincent Leroux; p.133 topVincent Leroux; bottom Vincent Leroux; p.134 Vincent Leroux; p.135 Vincent Leroux; p.136 Vincent Leroux; p.138 Vincent Leroux; p.139 Vincent Leroux; p.140 top Vincent Leroux; bottom Vincent Leroux; p.141 Vincent Leroux; p.142 Vincent Leroux; p.143 Vincent Leroux; p.144 Vincent Leroux; p.145 Vincent Leroux; p.146 left Vincent Leroux; right Vincent Leroux; p.147 top Vincent Leroux; bottom Vincent Leroux; p.148 Vincent Leroux

Cover pictures:

Top: Robert Harding Picture Library
Bottom: Paul Slaughter-The Image Bank